ANIMAL TRACKS AND HUNTER SIGNS

Copyright © 2017 Read Books Ltd.
This book is copyright and may not be
reproduced or copied in any way without
the express permission of the publisher in writing

British Library Cataloguing-in-Publication Data
A catalogue record for this book is available from the
British Library

Ernest Thompson Seton

Ernest Thompson Seton was born on 14th August 1860, in South Shields, County Durham, England. He grew up to be a pioneering author, wildlife artist, founder of the Woodcraft Indians, and one of the originators of the Boy Scouts of America (BSA).

The Seton family emigrated to Canada when Ernest was just six years old, and most of his childhood was consequently spent in Toronto. As a youth, he retreated to the woods to draw and study animals as a way of avoiding his abusive father – a practice which shaped the rest of his adult life. On his twenty-first birthday, Seton's father presented him with a bill for all the expenses connected with his childhood and youth, including the fee charged by the doctor who delivered him. He paid the bill, but never spoke to his father again.

Originally known as Ernest Evan Thompson, Ernest changed his name to Ernest Thompson Seton, believing that Seton had been an important name in his paternal line. He became successful as a writer, artist and naturalist, and moved to New York City to further his career. Seton later lived at 'Wyndygoul', an estate that he built in Cos Cob, a section of Greenwich, Connecticut. After experiencing vandalism by some local youths, Seton invited the young miscreants to his estate for a weekend, where he told them what he claimed were stories of the American Indians and of nature.

After this experience, he formed the Woodcraft Indians (an American youth programme) in 1902 and invited the local youth to join (at first just boys, but later girls as well). The stories that Seton told became a series of articles written for the *Ladies Home Journal*, and were eventually collected in *The Birch Bark Roll of the Woodcraft Indians* in 1906. Seton also met Scouting's founder, Lord Baden-Powell, in 1906. Baden-Powell had read Seton's book of stories, and was greatly intrigued by it. After the pair had met and shared ideas, Baden-Powell went on to found the Scouting movement worldwide, and Seton became vital in the foundation of the Boy Scouts of America (BSA) and was its first Chief Scout (from 1910 – 1915). Despite this large achievement, Seton quickly became embroiled in disputes with the BSA's other founders, Daniel Carter Beard and James E. West.

In addition to disputes about the content of Seton's contributions to the Boy Scout Handbook, conflicts also arose about the suffrage activities of his wife, Grace, and his British citizenship (it being *an American* organization). In his personal life, Seton was married twice. The first time was to Grace Gallatin in 1896, with whom he had one daughter, Ann (who later changed her name to Anya), and secondly to Julia M. Buttree, with whom he adopted an infant daughter, Beulah (who also changed her first name, to Dee). Alongside his work with the Woodcraft Indians and the BSA, Seton also found time to pursue his primary interest – that of nature writing.

Seton was an early pioneer of animal fiction writing, his most popular work being *Wild Animals I Have Known* (1898), which contains the story of his killing of the wolf Lobo. He later became involved in a literary debate known as the nature fakers controversy, after John Burroughs published an article in 1903 in the *Atlantic Monthly* attacking writers of sentimental animal stories. The controversy lasted for four years and included important

American environmental and political figures of the day, including President Theodore Roosevelt. Seton was also associated with the Santa Fe arts and literary community during the mid-1930s and early 1940s, which comprised a group of artists and authors including author and artist Alfred Morang, sculptor and potter Clem Hull, painter Georgia O'Keeffe, painter Randall Davey, painter Raymond Jonson, leader of the Transcendental Painters Group, and artist Eliseo Rodriguez.

In 1931, Seton became a United States citizen. He died on 23rd October, 1946 (aged eighty-six) in Seton Village in northern New Mexico. Seton was cremated in Albuquerque. In 1960, in honour of his 100th birthday and the 350th anniversary of Santa Fe, his daughter Dee and his grandson, Seton Cottier (son of Anya), in a fitting tribute to the man who loved his surrounding countryside so much, scattered his ashes over Seton Village from an airplane.

A few of the books by
ERNEST THOMPSON SETON

ANIMAL TRACKS AND HUNTER SIGNS
TRAIL OF AN ARTIST-NATURALIST
GREAT HISTORIC ANIMALS
GOSPEL OF THE REDMAN (with Julia M. Seton)
FAMOUS ANIMAL STORIES
LIVES OF GAME ANIMALS (4 volumes)
THE BOOK OF WOODCRAFT AND INDIAN LORE
WOODLAND TALES
THE PREACHER OF CEDAR MOUNTAIN
THE WOODCRAFT MANUAL FOR BOYS
WILD ANIMAL WAYS
THE WOODCRAFT MANUAL FOR GIRLS
WILD ANIMALS AT HOME
LIFE-HISTORIES OF NORTHERN ANIMALS
THE BIOGRAPHY OF A SILVER-FOX
ANIMAL HEROES
MONARCH, THE BIG BEAR OF TALLAC
TWO LITTLE SAVAGES
LIVES OF THE HUNTED
WILD ANIMALS I HAVE KNOWN
ROLF IN THE WOODS

Animal Tracks

Snapping Turtle

and
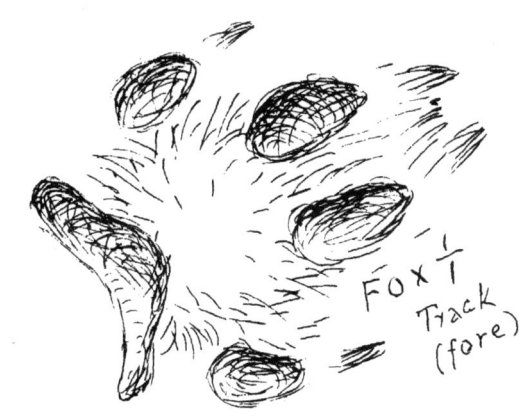
Hunter Signs

ERNEST THOMPSON SETON

NOTE TO THE READER

For over seventy years I have followed the Trail—in the backwoods of Canada, over the snows of Manitoba, through the swamps of Florida, on the sands of the Arctic tundra, in the level fields of England and of France, on the mountains of Norway; yes, and sometimes in the sedimentary rocks that one time were the mud, through which some bygone creature walked in the long ago.

My pleasure and reward have kept on ever increasing, as is always the case with one who earnestly follows a nature trail.

I have spent many days and many nights on the trail, following, following patiently, reading the life of the beast, using a notebook at every important move and change. Many an odd new sign has turned up to be put on record and explained by later experience.

Often a day passed with nothing tangible in the way of reward. Then, as in all hunting, there has come a streak of luck, a shower of facts and abundant compensation for

NOTE TO THE READER

the barren weeks gone by, an insight into animal ways and mind that could not have been obtained by any other method.

For here it is, written down by the animal itself, in the oldest of all writing, and recording a chapter when the creature was not escaping, but pursuing the placid even tenor of its normal forest life.

In this review of my observations, I have given track diagrams of many beasts, reptiles, and birds, all of them drawn from life and to scale, and all observed in America.

This is a mere start in trailing; I hope it may result in giving others as much joy as it has given me.

Ernest Thompson Seton
Seton Village
Santa Fe, New Mexico
August 14, 1946

N.B. The drawings and notes are taken wholly from the author's own lifelong experiences in the wilds; but the assembling of them into a readable book after Mr. Seton's death was done by his wife, Julia M. Seton who lived with him through many of the adventures that led to this writing.

Those drawings which the author made life size and marked correspondingly $\frac{1}{1}$ (e.g. page 41) have been reproduced in approximately three-quarters their original size.

Since Ernest Thompson Seton was an American writer, no attempt has been made to anglicize the spelling or vocabulary.

Contents

NOTE TO THE READER		vii
1.	The Oldest of All Writing	17
2.	Tracking, Trailing, or Spooring	23
3.	On Making Track Records	33
4.	The Coon That Taught Me How	39
5.	Black-Tracks	47
6.	Trailing as the Hunter Does It	51
7.	A Rabbit Adventure	59
8.	Around an Eastern Farm	69
9.	Marsh and Woodland Creatures	73
10.	Track History of Mink and Rabbit	77
11.	Record of a Woodland Tragedy	81
12.	Out West	87
13.	A Chapter of Fox Life	93
14.	Tracks in Town	101
15.	The Skunk and the Unwise Bobcat	105
16.	The Dude on the Trail	109
17.	Dabbles the Coon	111

18.	Deer and Antelope Tracks	115
19.	Some Northern Animals	119
20.	Scats or Signs	131
21.	Bear Trees and Other Animal Signs	143
22.	Blazes and Indian Signs	147
23.	Blazes Used in Town	155
A Final Word		157
INDEX		159

Illustrations

1. Tracks near the barn — 19
2. Woodland and marsh life — 21
3. Whitetail Deer tracks — 25
4. Deer in action — 27
5. Tracks on the farm — 29
6. Mountain Lion tracks — 31
7. Fox feet — 35
8. Various tracks of domestic Pig — 37
9. Domestic Sheep and Pig tracks compared — 38
10. Otter tracks — 41
11. Shod Horse walking — 43
12. Horse galloping and walking — 45
13. Black-track prints of Texan Lynx and Red Fox — 49
14. Black-tracks of Fox Squirrel and Meadow Mouse — 50
15. Birds on the ranch — 53
16. Tracks of domestic Cattle walking — 55
17. Dog and Wolf encounter at Buffalo skull — 57
18. Jack Rabbit and Cottontail tracks — 61
19. Rabbit labels — 63
20. Tracks of Rabbits — 65
21. Jack Rabbits frolicking — 67
22. Trails of Dog, Fox, and Cat — 70

ILLUSTRATIONS

23.	Turtle tracks in mud	75
24.	Tracks in the mud	76
25.	Mink on the Rabbit's trail	79
26.	A woodland tragedy	83
27.	Rabbits and Fox speeding	85
28.	Wolf, Coyote, and Fox	89
29.	A chapter of Fox life	95
30.	Tracks in town	103
31.	Human tracks	104
32.	The unwise Bobcat	106
33.	Tracks of Common Skunk	108
34.	Life of a Coon	112
35.	Various birds	114
36.	Tracks of Mule Deer	117
37.	Tracks of large Antelope	118
38.	Bull Moose and Possum tracks	120
39.	Moose tracks	121
40.	Musk Ox details	122
41.	Buffalo tracks and signs	123
42.	Tracks of Caribou	124
43.	Tracks of Bull Elk	125
44.	Tracks of Marten	126
45.	Paws of Marten	127
46.	Tracks of three large Bears	128
47.	Track record of Snowshoe Hare	129
48.	Scatology of the Deer	133
49.	Scatology of certain Rodents	135
50.	Scatology of certain Mustelidae	137
51.	Muskrat post office	141
52.	Animal signs	145
53.	Blazes and Indian signs	149
54.	Blazes used in town	156

THE TRAILER

Blest with a Magic Power is he,
  Drinks deep where others sipped;
And Wild Things write their lives for him
  In endless manuscript.

ANIMAL TRACKS AND HUNTER SIGNS

1 The Oldest of All Writing

"I wish I could go West and join the Indians so that I should have no lessons to learn," said an unhappy small boy who could discover no atom of sense or purpose in any one of the three Rs.

"You never made a greater mistake," replied the scribe, "for the young Indian has many lessons to learn from his earliest days—hard lessons and hard punishments.

"With him the dread penalty of failure is 'go hungry till you win'; and no more important task has he than his reading lesson.

"Not just twenty-six characters are to be learned in this exercise, but a thousand. Not clear straight print are these characters, but dim, washed-out, crooked traces. Not indoors on comfortable chairs are the lessons, with a wise and patient teacher always near, but out in the forest, often alone, and in every kind of weather.

"There he slowly deciphers the letters and reads sentences of the oldest writing on earth—a style so old that the hieroglyphs of Egypt, the cylinders of Nippur, and the drawings of the cave men are as things of today in comparison; a writing indeed that is older than mankind, the one universal script. I mean the tracks in the dust, the mud, or the snow.

"These are the inscriptions that every hunter, Red or White, must learn to read infallibly. And, be the writing strong or faint, straight or crooked, simple or overwritten with many a puzzling diverse phrase, he must decipher and follow swiftly, unerringly, if there is to be a successful ending to the hunt which provides his daily food."

This is the reading lesson of the young Indian, and it is a style that will never become superseded.

The naturalist also must acquire some measure of proficiency in the ancient art. Its usefulness is perennial to the student of wildlife; without it he would know little of the people of the wood.

It is a remarkable fact that there are always more wild animals about than any but the expert has any idea of. For example there are, within twenty miles of New York City, fully fifty different kinds, not counting birds, reptiles, or fishes, at least one quarter of which are abundant. Or, more particularly, within the limits of Greater New York, living their free and normal lives, there are at least a dozen species of wild beasts, half of which are quite common.

To illustrate: along the shores of Staten Island and Long Island one will surely find Mink, Muskrat, and Coon, not to mention Bats. In the woods will be Gray Squirrels, Red Squirrels, Flying Squirrels, Chipmunks, Moles, and Shrews. Around the farms and other homes, House Rats, House Mice, and Deer Mice would abound. Possums, Woodchucks, Skunks, and Weasels are occasional, and a number of others make their appearance here and there.

"Then how is it that we never see any?" is the first ques-

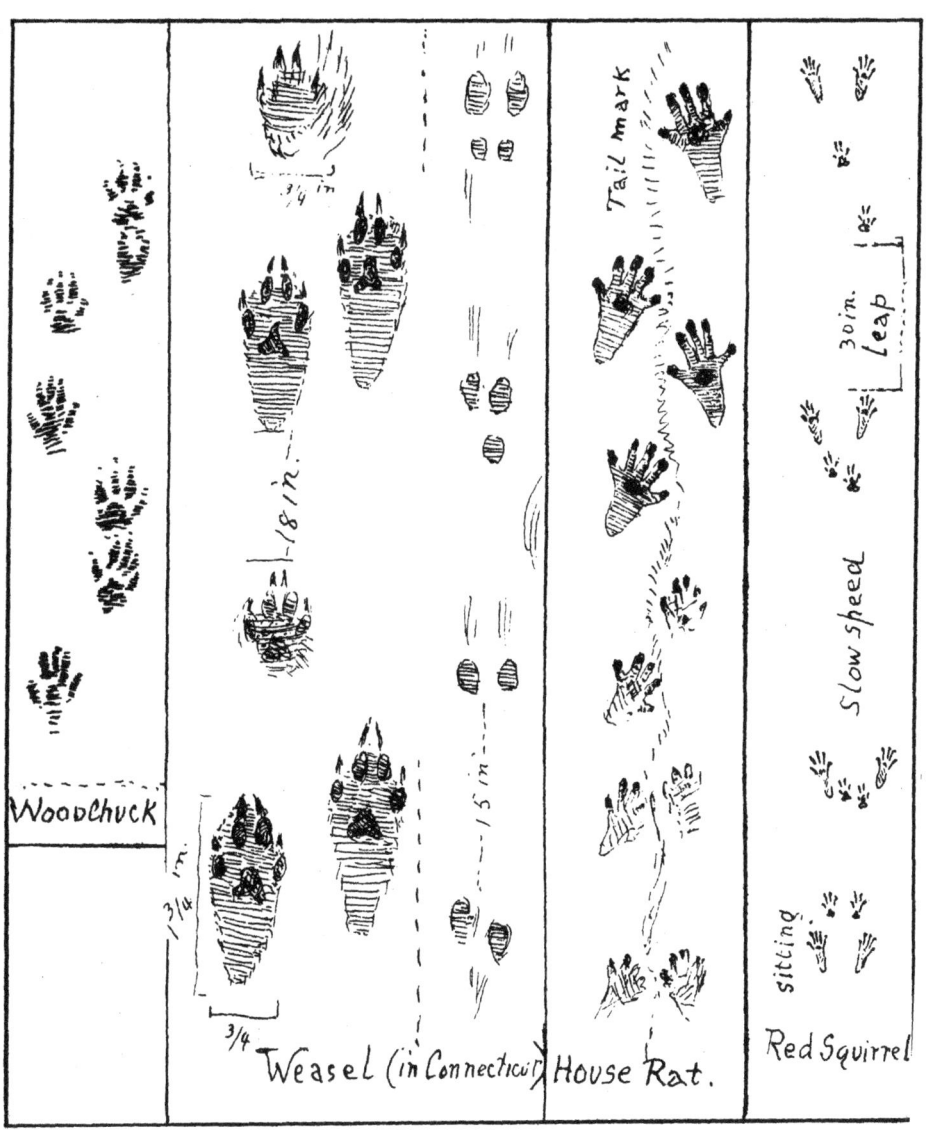

Tracks near the barn

tion of the incredulous. The answer is simple.

Long ago the beasts learned this dire lesson: Man is your worst enemy; shun him at any price. And the simplest way to do this is to come out only at night. Man is a daytime creature; he is blind in the soft half-light or darkness that most beasts prefer.

While many animals have always limited their activity to the hours of twilight and gloom, there are not a few that were once diurnal, but have given up that portion of their working day in order to avoid the archenemy, man.

Thus they can flourish under our noses, and eat at our tables, without our consent or even knowledge. They come and go at will, and the world knows nothing of them. Their presence might long be unsuspected, but for one thing, well known to the hunter, the trapper, and the naturalist. WHEREVER THE WILD FOURFOOT GOES, IT LEAVES BEHIND IT A DETAILED RECORD OF ITS VISIT. This it puts down in the ancient script of the woods, the script of the footmark trail, the story of at least a portion of its life.

Each of these dotted lines is a wonderful record of the creature's activity during the time it was there. It needs only the patient work of the seeker to decipher that record and from it learn much about the animal that made it; yes, even without that animal ever having been seen by him.

Savages are more skilled in this art than are civilized folk, for tracking is their serious lifelong pursuit, and they have not injured their eyes with books. Intelligence is, indeed, important here as elsewhere; yet it is a remarkable fact that the lowest race of mankind, the Australian blacks, are reputed to be by far the best trackers. Not only are their eyes and attention developed and disciplined, but they have retained much of the scent power that civilized man has lost. They can follow a fresh track, partly at least, by smell.

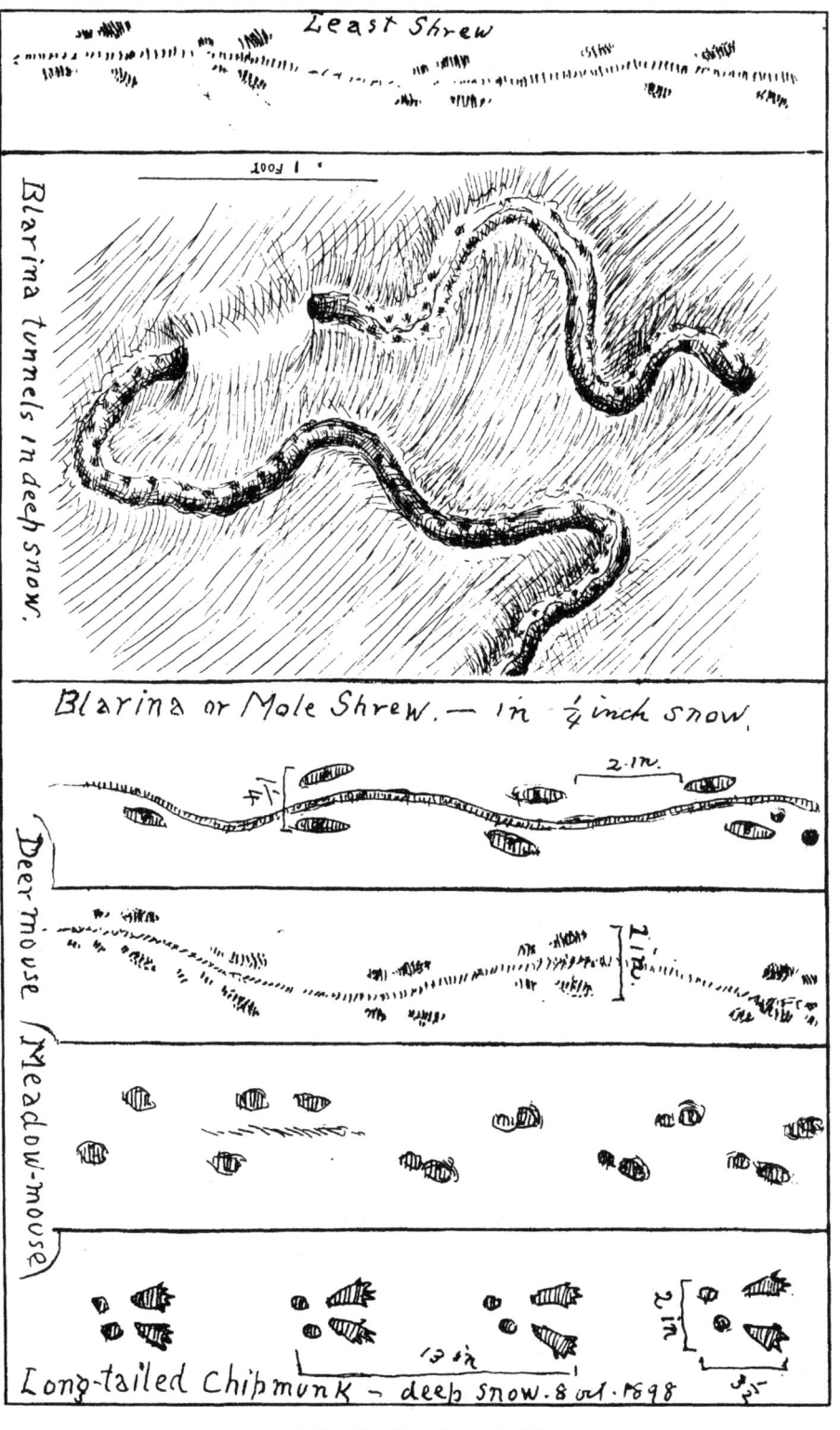

Woodland and marsh life

2 Tracking, Trailing, or Spooring

The first lesson of a young hunter, after knowing the animals themselves, is recognizing their tracks. He must not only recognize them, however; he must learn to follow them and read the information that they offer.

As I have already said, tracks are the oldest writing in the world. We have track records that are millions of years old; the track is there long after the creature that made it is dead and gone, even wholly extinct.

But the most useful track records for us today are those that we find in the dust, or better still the snow.

Since the trail is the unquestionable story of the wild being at that time, one should lose no chance to study and record the tracks of animals if he wishes to be a real naturalist.

Whether one specializes in birds, beasts, stars, diseases, microbes, metals, or tracks, the first step in knowledge is *exact identification.*

The expert hunter after quadrupeds that frequent the

woods gets information and guidance from passing glimpses of the animal, the information supplied by the dung pellets, the marks that it makes in feeding on or scratching the bark and brush of trees, the sounds that it makes by voice or by attacks on tree trunks, the cries of birds that are aroused by its presence and call in protest or in signal to other birds.

But by far the most important sources of information are the tracks that the creature makes as it travels or maneuvers in the soft earth, the mud, or the snow of its haunts. The tracks tell exactly when and where the creature passed, its species, its size and mood, whether old or young, sometimes even its sex, whether alarmed and flying for safety, or dozing in calm repose. It tells all about the animal, and more fully than in any other way, except by a clear view close at hand —such a view indeed as is rarely secured for more than a few seconds, while the track record covers the life of the creature for hours, sometimes for days.

It is hard to overvalue the power of the skillful tracker. To him the trail of each animal is not a mere series of similar footprints; it is an accurate account of the creature's ways, habits, changing whims, and emotions during the portion of life of which the record is in view. These are indeed autobiographical chapters and differ from some other autobiographies in this—*they cannot tell a lie.* We may get wrong information from them, but it is our own fault if we do; we misread the unimpeachable document.

Furthermore, under the proper conditions, the track record is imperishable. We need not be on the spot when the writings were made. We have in the rocks today track stories that were told, then in the mud, a million years before man appeared on this planet.

The ideal time for tracking, and almost the only time for

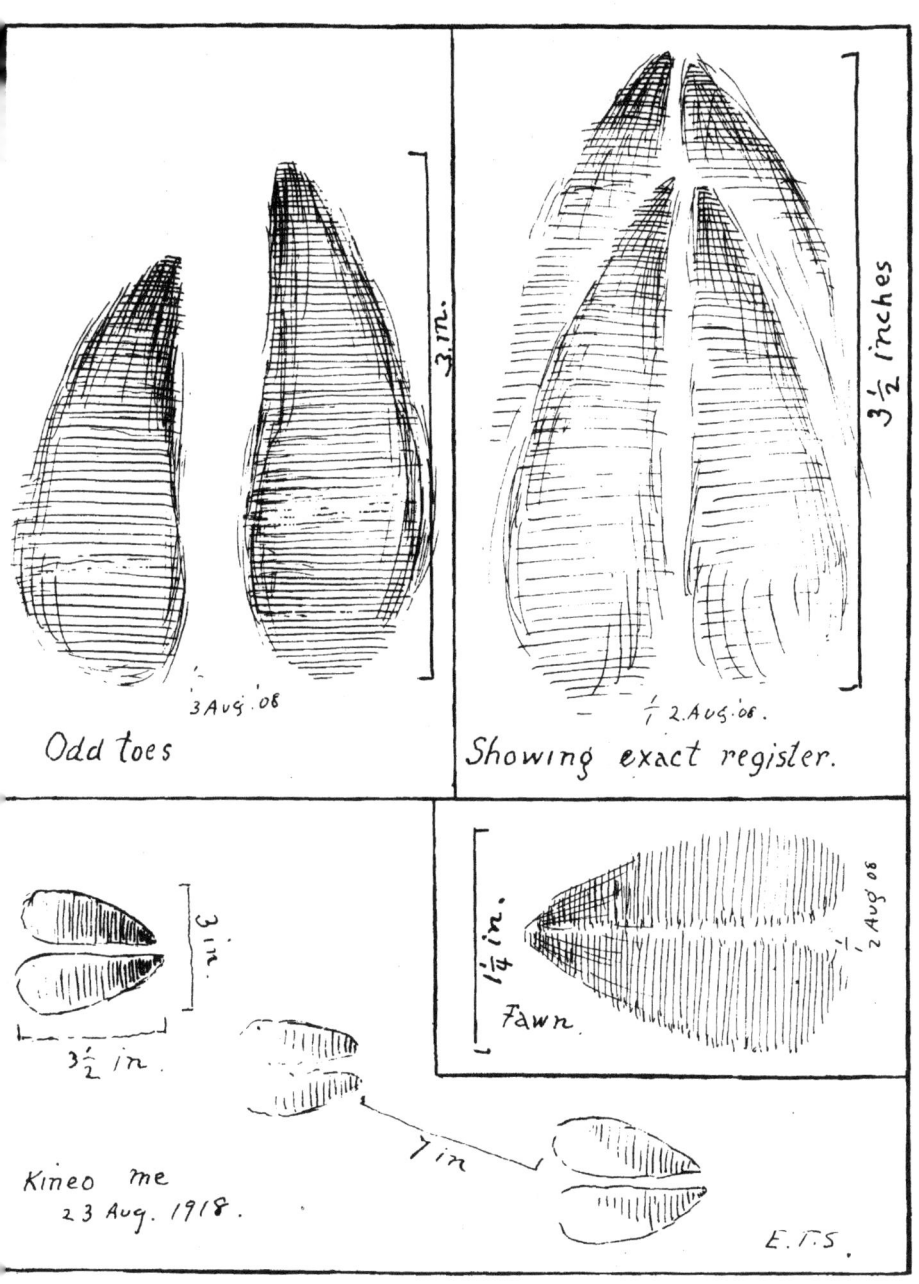

Whitetail Deer tracks

most folk, is when the ground is white. After the first snow the student walks forth and begins at once to realize the wonders of the trail. A score of creatures whose existence, maybe, he did not know of are now revealed all about him, and the reading of their life histories becomes easy.

It is when the snow is on the ground, indeed, that we take the census of the woods. How often we learn with surprise from the telltale white that a Fox was around our hen house last night, that a Mink is living even now under the woodpile, or that a Deer—yes! there is no mistaking its sharp-pointed unsheeplike footprint—has wandered into our woods from the farther wilds!

Never lose the chance of the first snow if you wish to become a trailer. Nevertheless, remember that the first morning after a night snowfall is not so good as the second, for most wild creatures "hole up" during the storm; the snow hides the tracks of those that do go forth; and some actually go into a "cold sleep" for a day or two after a heavy downfall accompanied by severe frost. But a calm, mild night following a storm is sure to offer abundant and ideal opportunity for beginning the study of the trail.

It is a most fascinating amusement to learn some creature's way of life by following its fresh track for hours in good snow. I never miss such a chance. If I cannot find a fresh track, I take a stale one, knowing that, theoretically, it is fresher at every step, and, from practical experience, that it always eventually brings one to some track that *is* fresh.

Although so much is to be read in the wintry white, we cannot at that time make a full account of all the woodland fourfoots, for there are some kinds that do not come out in the snow; they sleep more or less all winter.

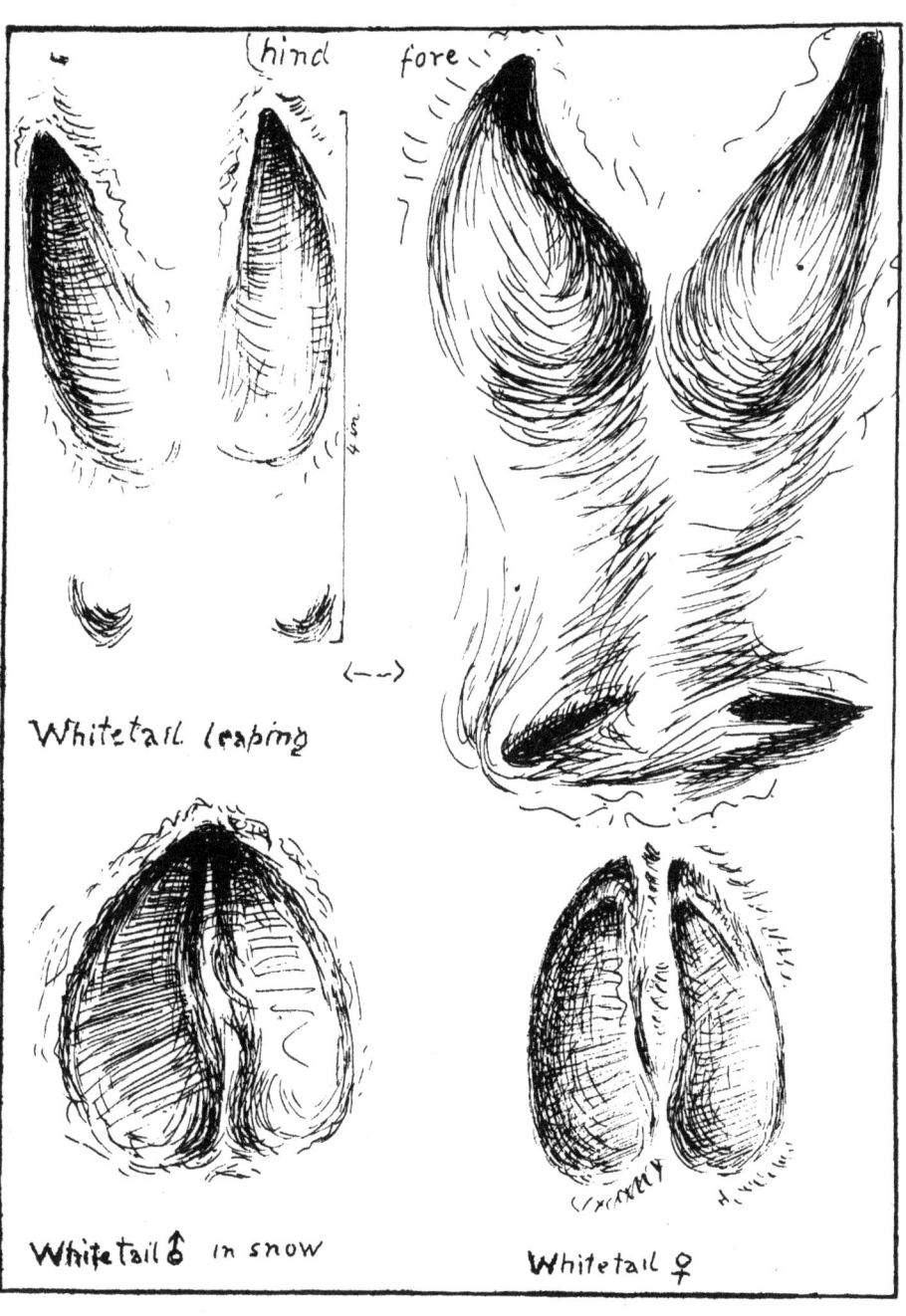

Deer in action

Thus, one rarely sees the track of Chipmunk or Woodchuck in truly winter weather; and never, so far as I know, have the trails of Jumping Mouse or Mud Turtle been seen in the snow. These we can track only in the mud or dust.

Such tracks cannot be followed as far as those in snow, simply because the mud or dust does not cover the whole country; but they are often as clear and in some respects more easy of record.

Here are some of the important facts to keep in view when you set forth to master the rudiments of trailing, or "spooring," as our English friends call it.

FIRST: No two animals leave the same trail; not only each kind but each individual at each stage of its life leaves a trail as distinctive as the creature's appearance. It is obvious that they differ among themselves just as do we, because the young know their mothers, the mothers know their young, and the old ones know their mates, even when scent is clearly out of the question.

SECOND: The trail in its entirety was begun at the birthplace of that creature, and ends only at its death. It may be recorded in visible track or perceptible odor. It may last but a few hours and may be too faint even for an expert with present equipment to follow. But evidently the trail is made, wherever the creature journeys afoot.

THIRD: It varies with every important change of impulse, action, and emotion.

FOURTH: When we find a trail we may rest assured that, if living, *the creature that made it is at the other end;* and if one can follow, it is only a question of time before coming up with that animal. But be sure of its direction before setting out; many a novice has lost time by going backward on the trail.

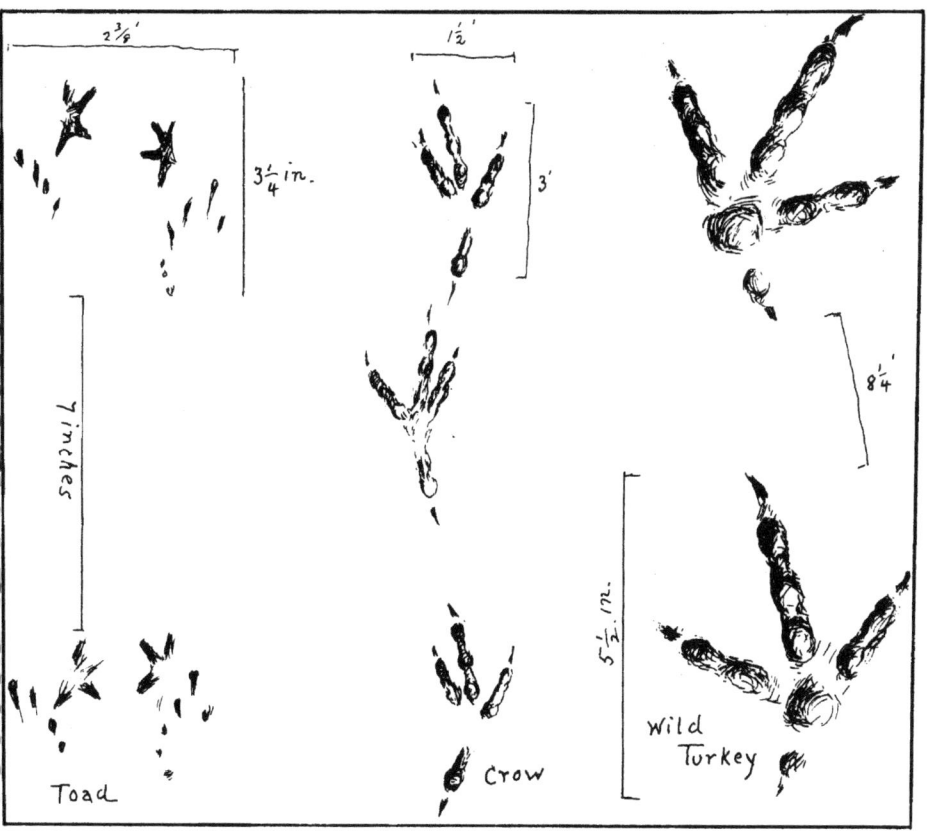

Tracks on the farm

A practical trailer can, of course, tell something of the trail's age by careful study. This finesse, however, is usually beyond the power of the beginner.

FIFTH: In studying trails, one must always keep probabilities in mind. Sometimes one kind of track looks much like another; then the question is, which is the likeliest in this place?

If I saw a Jaguar track in India, I should know it was made by a Leopard. If I found a Leopard trail in Colorado, I should be sure I had found the mark of a Cougar or Mountain Lion. A Wolf track on Broadway would doubtless be the work of a very large Dog; and a Saint Bernard's footmark in the Rockies, twenty miles from anywhere, would most likely turn out to be the happen-so imprint of a Gray Wolf's foot. To be sure of the marks, then, one should know all the animals that belong to the neighborhood.

The last letter I had from good old Dan Beard contained the photo of a track in the snow that he recently found under his bedroom window at Suffern, New York. He asked me to identify it for him.

The track was catlike in type, but too big for a House Cat. Therefore, it was either a Lynx or a Bobcat sign. It was not clear enough to show the exact style of the creature's foot; but locality settled it. Bobcats are the usual kind of Lynx in southern New York; the Canada Lynx is now unknown in the region. So we concluded that the geographical placement definitely decided it to be a Bobcat or Bay Lynx that had peered by night into Uncle Dan's window as he lay calmly asleep.

There is yet another feature of trail study that gives it exceptional value: it is an account of the creature pursuing

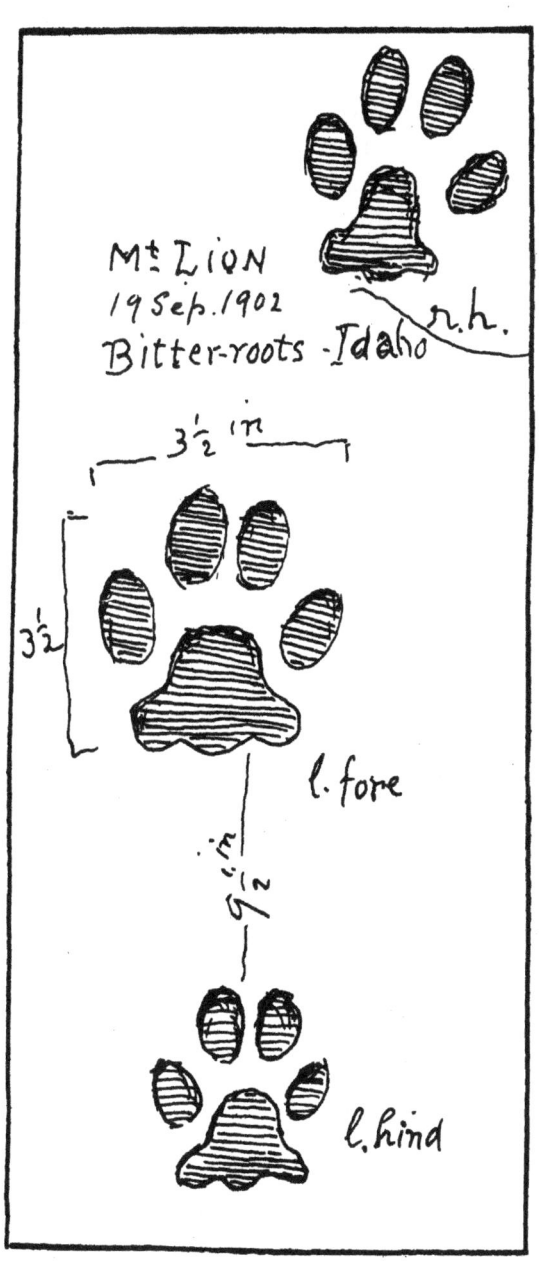

Mountain Lion tracks

its *everyday* life. If you succeed in getting a glimpse of a Fox or a Hare in the woods, the chances are a hundred to one that it was aware of your presence first. Animals are much cleverer than are we at this sort of thing; and if they do not actually sight or scent you, they observe, and are warned by, the actions of some other creatures that did sense you, and so cease their occupations to steal away or hide.

But the snow story will tell of the life that the animal ordinarily leads—its method of searching for food, its kinds of food, the help it gets from its friends, or sometimes from its rivals; and thus offers an insight into its home life that is scarcely to be attained in any other way. The trailer has the key to a new storehouse of nature's secrets, another of the Sibylline Books is opened to his view; his fairy godmother has, indeed, conferred on him a wonderful gift in opening his eyes to the footwriting of the trail. It is like giving sight to the blind man, like the rolling away of fogs from a mountain view; and the trailer comes closer than do others to the heart of the ancient woods.

3 On Making Track Records

There are four principal ways of making a record of tracks to facilitate comparison and identification.

First, and most usual, is by making a drawing. This method is best for hasty work, for passing opportunities, for a long series of tracks and for faint features or bad light. In fact, the drawing alone can give you everything you can perceive. Drawing is always possible, no matter what the light or the surroundings; but it can fail in authenticity of size and detail.

All my earliest attempts were in freehand drawing. It does answer, but has this great disadvantage: it is a translation, a record colored by an intervening personality; and the value of the result is likely to be limited by one's own knowledge at the time, as well as by one's skill in the technique of drawing.

In order to at least partially offset some of these disadvantages, it is well to have your drawing exactly life-size. For instance, it is only by the size that one can, as a rule, distinguish the trails of Wolf, Dog, Coyote, and Red Fox. There *are* other differences; but they are very minute, and discernible only to the keenest of eyes and in the clearest-cut tracks.

Second, photography naturally suggests itself, but the difficulties prove as great as they are unexpected. Not more than one track in a thousand is fit to photograph; the essential details are almost always left out.

For a really successful photograph you must have a clear, sharp track in the open, and you must have bright sunlight. Yet even when the weather is perfect there are practically but two times each day when it is possible, in midmorning and in midafternoon, when the sun is high enough for clear photographs and low enough to cast a shadow in the faint track, and thus achieve absolute definition. Sometimes good photos are made of tracks in dust and mud, as well as thick sticky snow, but rarely in powdery or very deep snow.

The great advantage of photography is the fact that it gives the surroundings, the essential landscape and the setting; therefore, the local reason for many changes of action on the part of the animal. Furthermore, the aesthetic beauties of its records are unique and will help to keep the method in a high place.

Third, by casting in plaster of Paris. This has the advantage of accuracy in three dimensions. But not one track in ten thousand is fit to cast; nearly all are blemished and imperfect in some way. And the most abundant—those in snow—cannot be cast at all. Besides, the method presupposes some cumbersome apparatus and an expert caster. Such tracks are difficult to store or to multiply; neverthe-

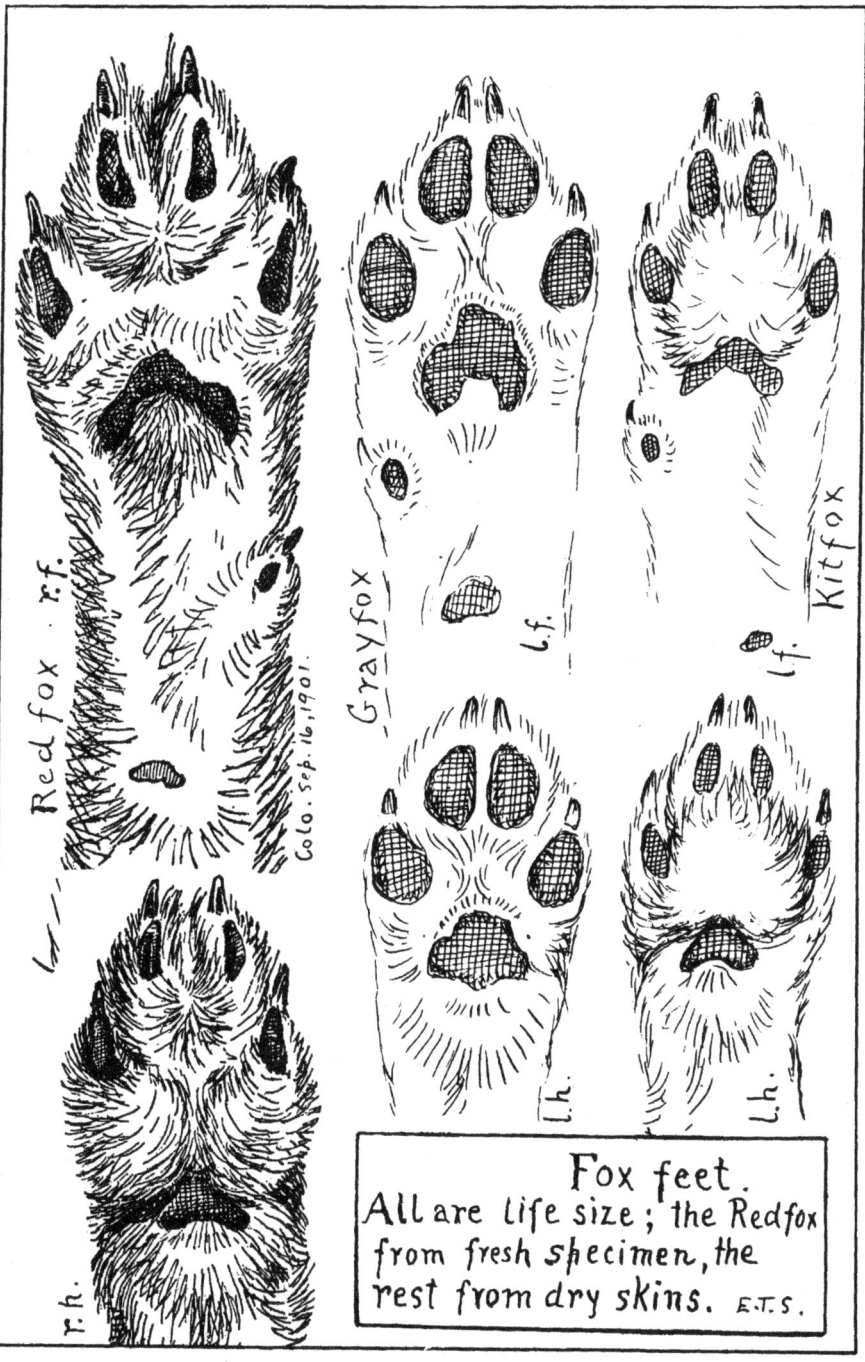

Fox feet. All are life size; the Redfox from fresh specimen, the rest from dry skins. E.T.S.

less are of much service, especially when a very clear mud track is found.

Fourth, by making a black-track record or print, using ink of some sort, and the paw of the animal as the printer's block. How to manage this is a problem, as we shall see in the next chapter.

As a variation of this method, I tried spreading plastic wax where the beasts would walk on it in pathways or before dens. How they did scoff! The simplest Ground Squirrel knew too much to venture on my waxen snare. *Around* it, or, if hemmed in, *over* it, with a mighty bound they went; but never a track did I so secure.

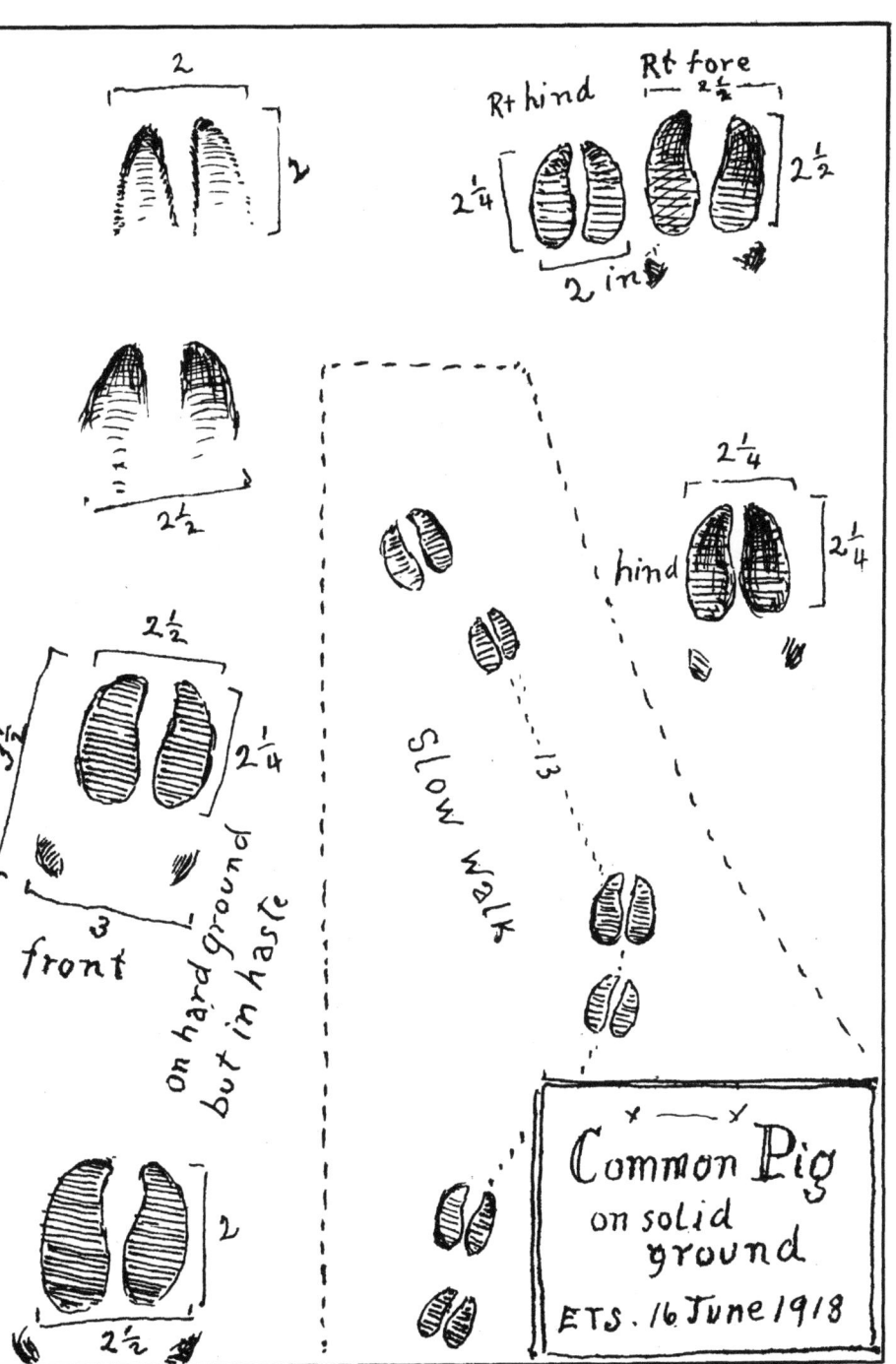

Various tracks of domestic Pig

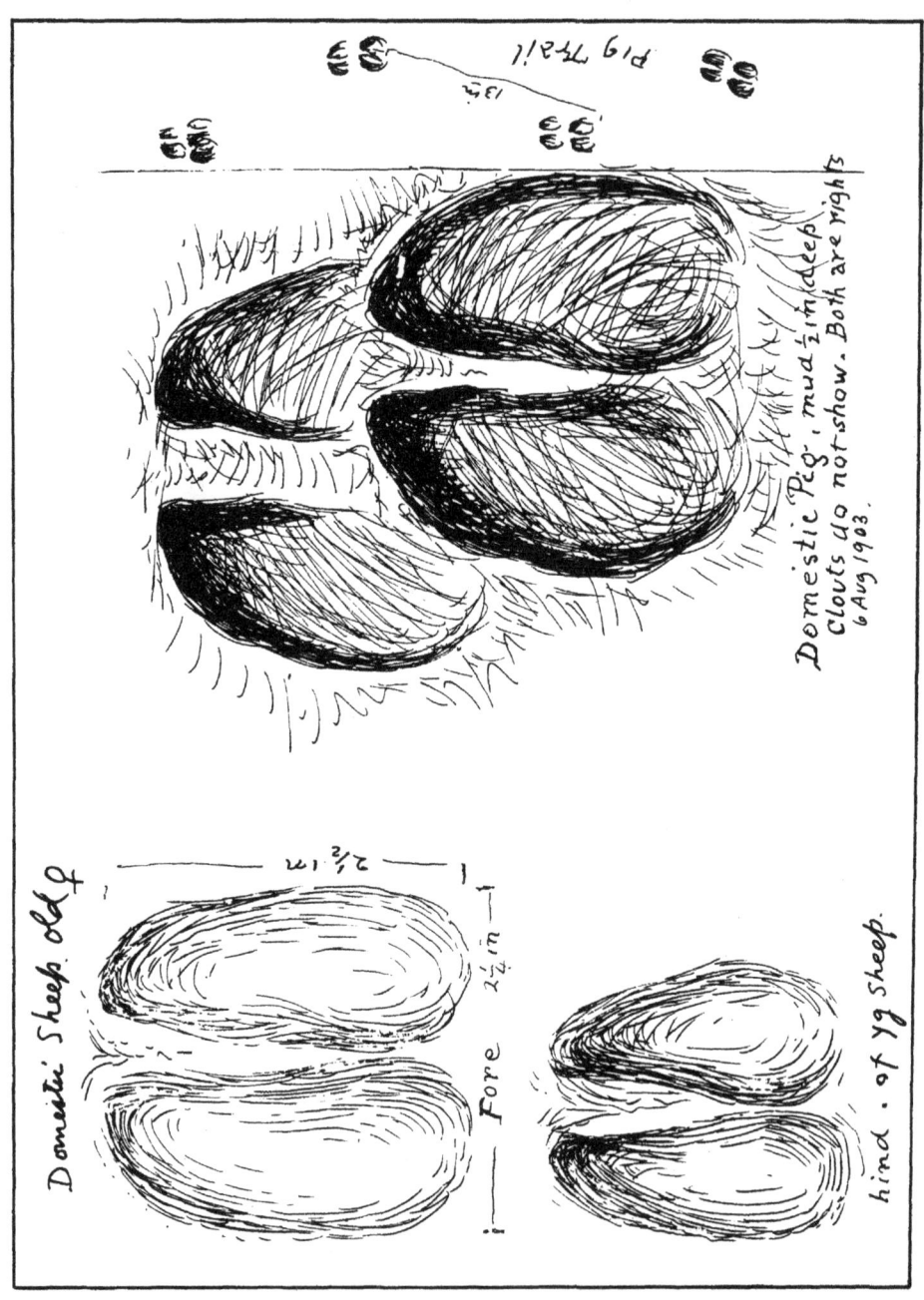

Domestic Sheep and Pig tracks compared

4 The Coon That Taught Me How

In the early days of my track study I searched for a perfect means of transferring wildlife tales to paper, or otherwise making a permanent collection of the tracks. As already told, photography and plaster casts suggested themselves, but all were subject to some serious objection.

Then a new method was presented in an unexpected way.

A friend of mine had a pet Raccoon, which he kept in a cage in his bachelor quarters uptown. One day, during my friend's absence, the Coon got loose and set about a series of long-deferred exploring expeditions, beginning with the bachelor's bedroom.

The first promising object was a writing desk. Mounting by a chair, the Coon examined several uninteresting books and papers, and then noticed higher up a large stone bottle. He had several times found pleasurable stuff in bottles, so he went for that.

The cork was lightly in and easily disposed of. But the smell was far from inviting, for it was merely a quart of ink. Determined to leave no stone unturned, however, the Coon upset the ink to taste and try. Alas! It tasted even worse than it smelled; it was an utter failure as a beverage.

Then the Coon, pushing it contemptuously away, turned his attention to a pile of fine handmade deckle-edged heraldry note paper, the pride of my friend's heart; and when he raised his inky little paws, there were left on the paper some beautiful black prints. This was a new idea; the Coon tried it again and again.

But the ink held out longer than the paper; so the fur-clad printer worked over sundry books and the adjoining walls, while the ink, dribbling over everything, formed a great pool below the desk.

Something attracted the animal's attention, causing him to jump down. He landed in the pool of ink, making it splash in all directions. Some of the black splotches reached the white counterpane of the bachelor's bed. Another happy idea!

The Coon now leaped on the bed, racing around as long as the ink on his feet gave results. While he paused to rest, or perhaps to see if any place had been neglected, the door opened, and in came the landlady.

The scene which followed was too painful for description; no one present enjoyed it. My friend was sent for, to come and take his Coon out of there *forever*.

He came and took him away, I suppose "forever." He had only one other place for the creature—his office. And there it was I made the animal's acquaintance and heard of his exploit—an ink-and-paper, if not a literary affair.

This gave me the hint I needed, a plan to make an authentic record of animal tracks. Armed with printer's ink and paper rolls, I set about gathering a collection of imprints.

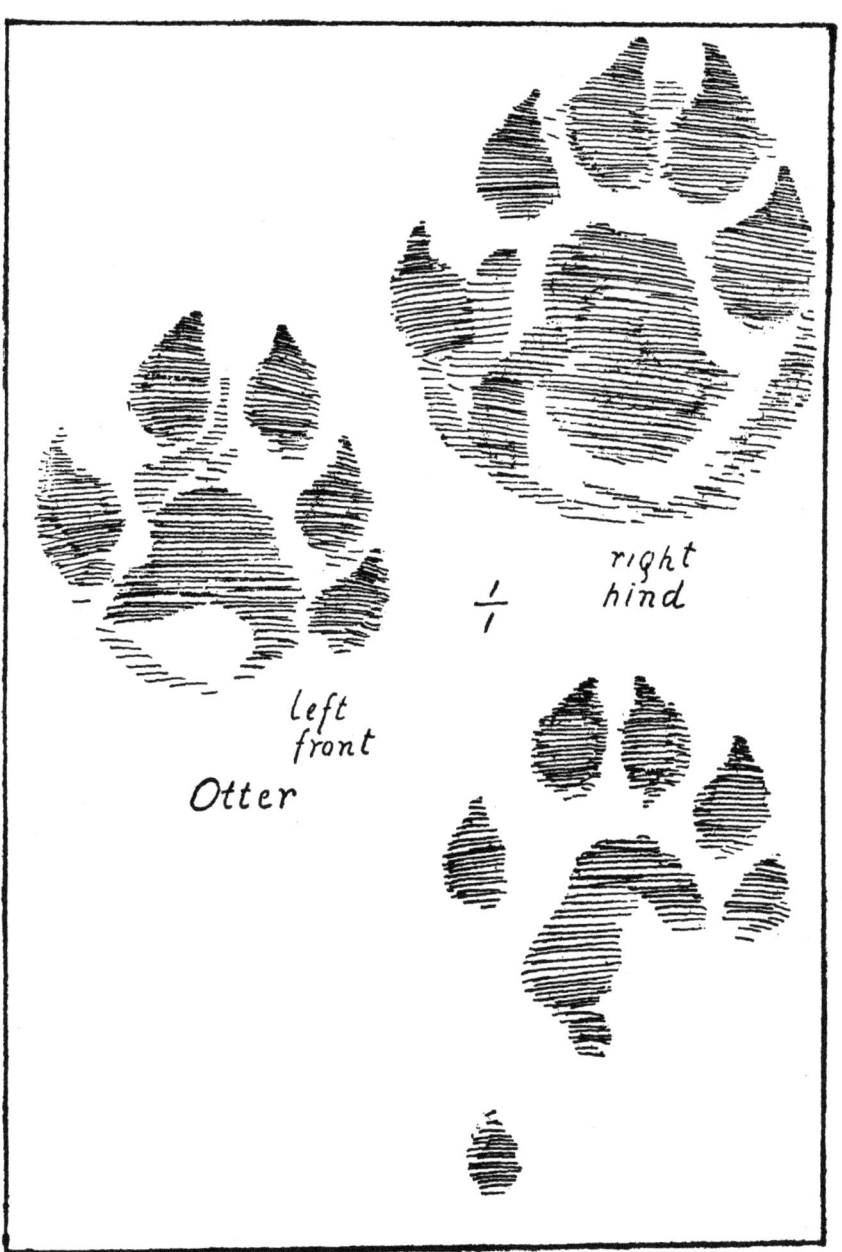

Otter tracks from caged specimen in Washington Zoo

After many failures and much experiment, better methods were devised. One was the substitution of black paint for printer's ink, as the latter dries too quickly. Another was padding under the paper, which should be light and soft for very light animals, and stronger and harder for the heavy. Printing from a Mouse, for instance, is much like printing a delicate etching; ink, paper, dampness, etc., must be exactly right. Furthermore, you have this handicap—you cannot regulate the pressure.

This is, of course, strictly a zoo method; all attempts to secure black prints from animals at large have been total failures. The paper, the smell of paint, etc., are enough to keep the wild things away.

In the zoo we spread the black pad and the white paper in a narrow, temporary lane, and drive, or try to drive, the captives over them, one by one, securing a series of tracks that are life-size, properly spaced, absolutely authentic, and capable of yielding more facts as the observer learns more about the subject.

As related here, all this sounds quite easy. But no one has any idea of how cross-crooked and contrary a creature can be, until he wishes it to repeat for him some ordinary thing that it has hitherto done hourly. Some of the animals balk at the paint, some at the paper, some make a leap to clear all, and thereby wreck the entire apparatus. Some will begin very well, but rush back when halfway over, so as to destroy the prints already made; and in most cases the calmest, steadiest, tamest of beasts becomes utterly wild, erratic, and unmanageable when approached with trackological intent.

Even domestic animals are difficult. A tame Cat that was highly trained to do anything a Cat could do was selected as

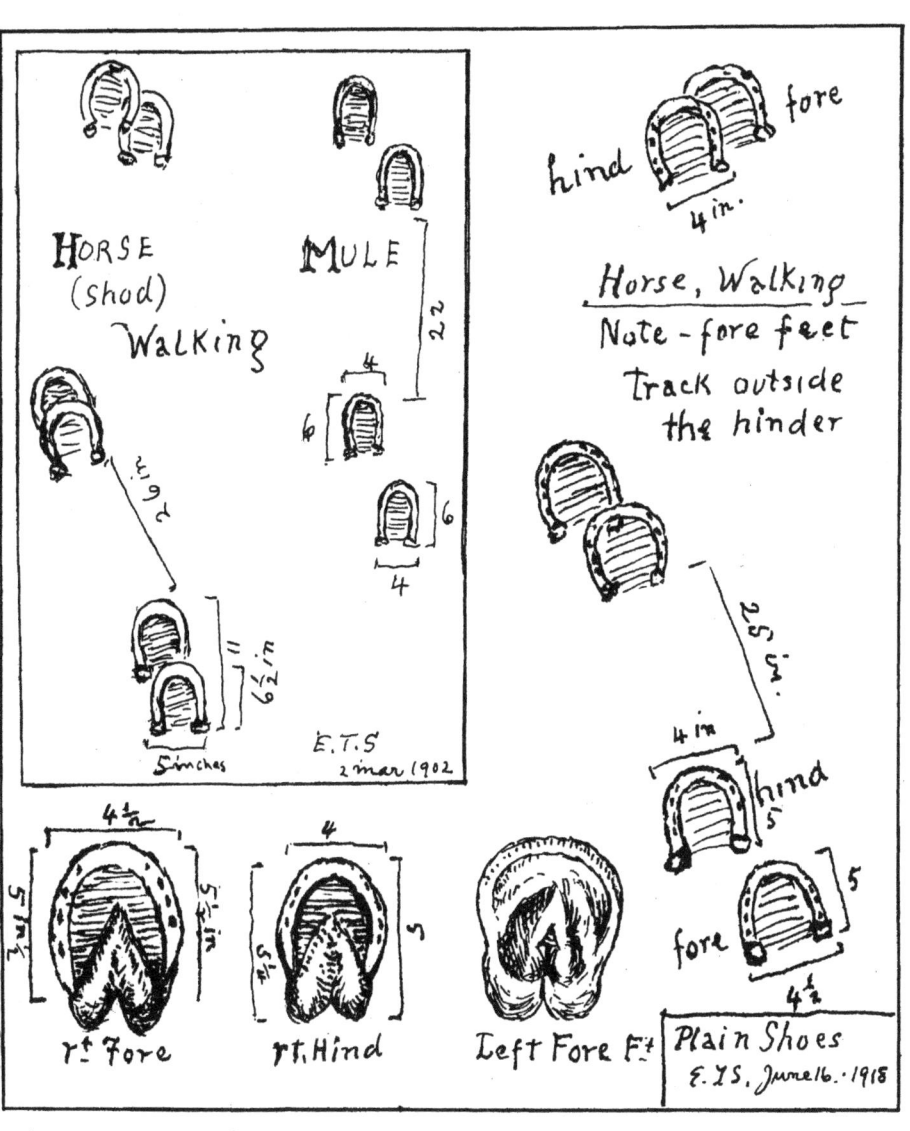

Shod Horse walking

promising for a black-track study, and her owner's two boys volunteered to get all the Cat tracks I needed. They put down a long roll of paper in a hall, painted Pussy's feet black, and proceeded to chase her up and down. Her docility vanished under the strain. She raced madly about, leaving long, useless splashes of black; then, leaping to a fanlight, she escaped upstairs to take refuge among the snowy draperies. After which, the boys' troubles began.

These, however, are mere by-incidents, and illustrate the many practical difficulties. After these are conquered with patience and ingenuity, there can be no doubt of the value of the prints.

Briefly, then, black-tracks are best for records of size, spacing, and detail, but fail wholly to give incidents of wildlife or landscape surroundings.

Thus, each of the four methods may be successful in a different way; and the best, most nearly perfect alphabet of the woods would include all four, consisting of a drawing, a cast, a pedoscript, and a photograph of each footprint, also a trail, i.e., the long series of footprints left by each animal.

My practice has been to use all whenever I could. Still, I find freehand drawing is the one of most practical application. When I do get a photograph I treasure it as an adjunct to the sketch.

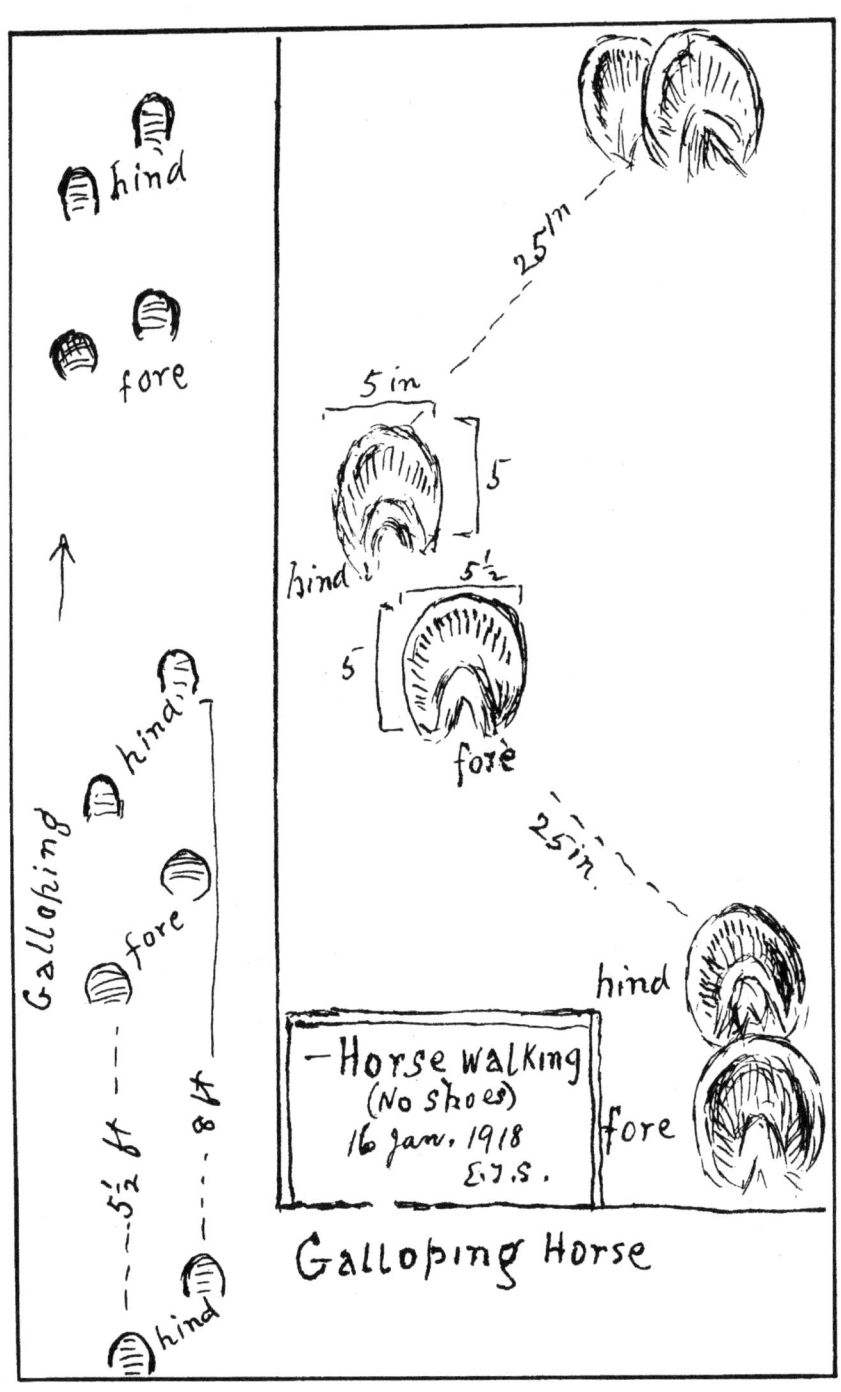

Horse galloping and walking

5 Black-Tracks

For over seventy years now I have been making records of such tracks as came my way. As a result, a couple of thousand drawings of tracks and trails are now in my collection; and of these less than 1 per cent were made with the black-tracking method. But before leaving the subject, I shall offer four illustrations of the same.

On page 49 at the top are prints made from the feet of a young Texan Lynx that was the household pet of a friend. These illustrate two important Cat features: the total absence of claws in the track; and the deep indentations at the back edge of the heel pad in each. The Dog's tracks are usually without these.

The two lower prints are from the right front and right hind pads of an American Red Fox in the Bronx Zoo. The Fox, being of Dog kinship, shows the claws in the track, and yet shows Cat affinities in the indentation at the back edge of the front paw.

On page 50 is illustrated the remarkable development of

toe pads, or shock absorbers, in the Fox Squirrel. The Squirrel landed as shown by the four tracks together at the lower part of the print; then, stopping to rest, he set the fore feet farther ahead.

The inset at the upper left side is the autographed black-track of the Short-tailed Meadow Mouse (*Microtus*). At first these dots look inconsequent and fortuitous; but a careful examination shows that the creature had four toes with claws on the fore feet, and five on the hind—which is evidence, though not conclusive, that it was a rodent. The absence of tail marks shows that the tail was short or wanting. The tubercles on each palm tell to which group of Mice the creature belongs. The alternation of the tracks shows that it was a ground animal, not a tree climber; the spacing indicates the shortness of the legs; their size determines the size of the creature.

Thus, we come near to reconstructing the animal from its tracks. We see how, by the help of such studies, we can get much light on bygone animals whose only monuments are tracks in the sedimentary rocks about us—rocks that, when they received these imprints, were the muddy margin of these long-gone creatures' haunts.

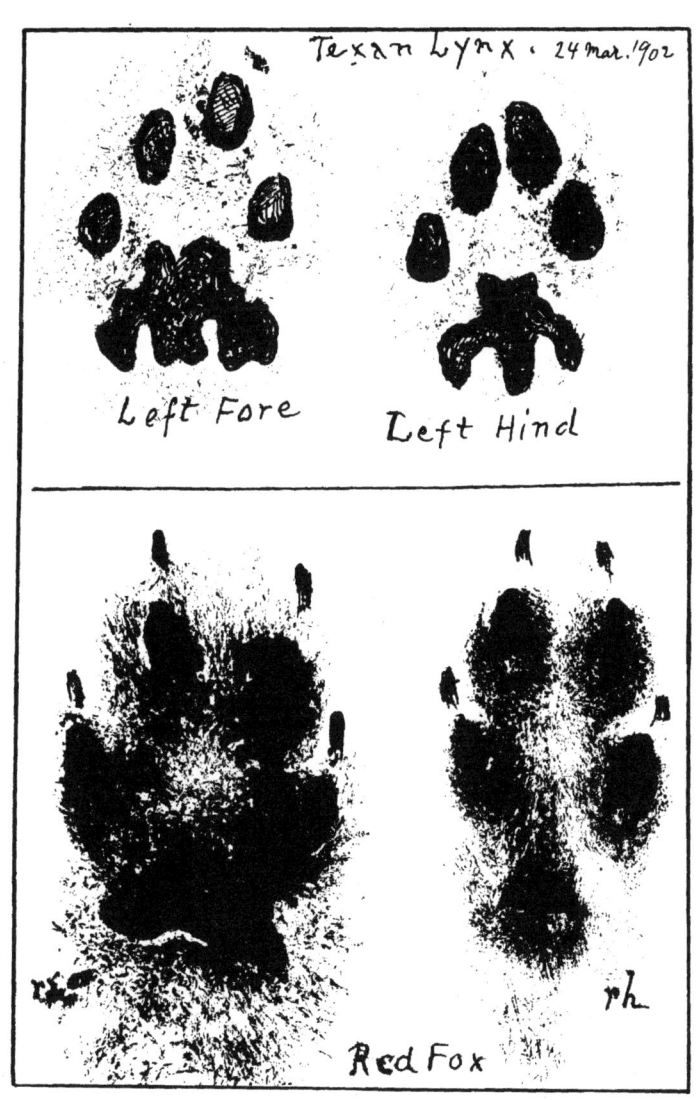

Black-track prints of Texan Lynx and Red Fox

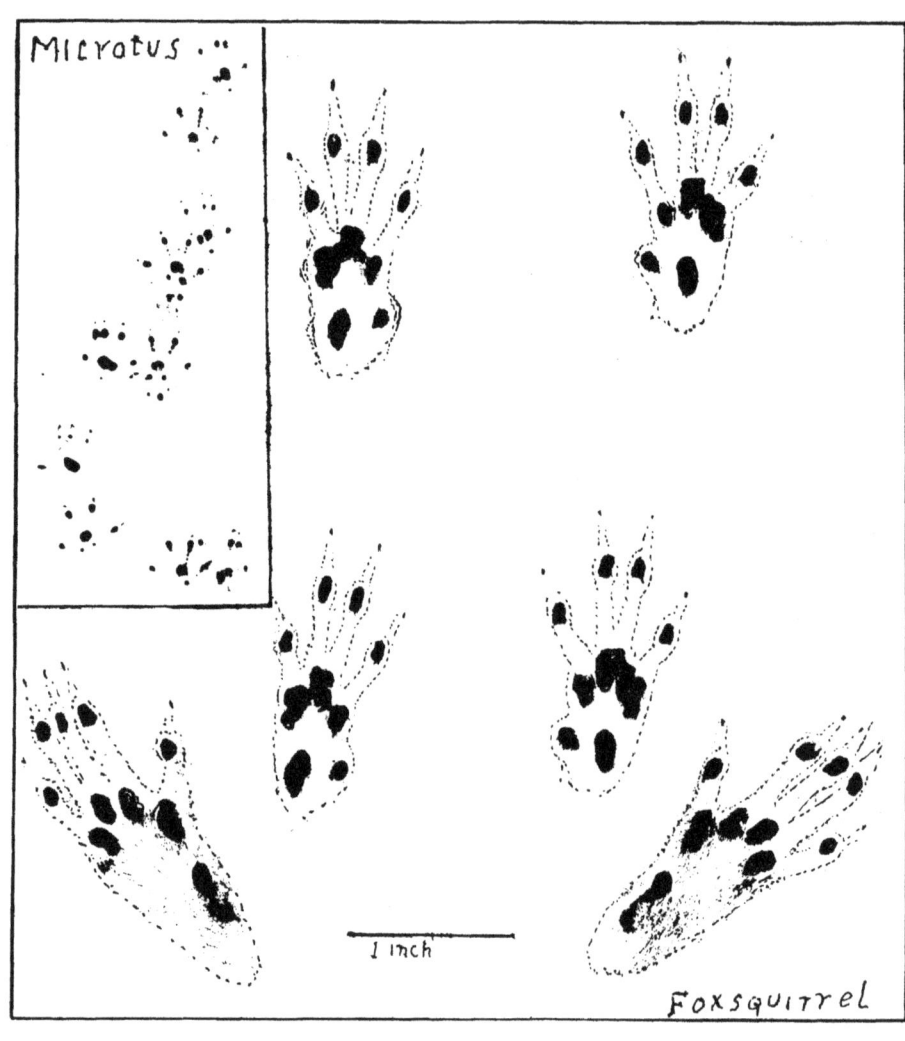

Black tracks of Fox Squirrel, with line added around each to show the position of the pads or shock absorbers. In the upper left corner are the black tracks of the Short-tailed Meadow Mouse (Microtus).

6   Trailing as the Hunter Does It

What is trailing?

The Fox hunter has some idea of it when he sees a superb pack follow a faint scent through a hundred perplexing places, discerning just which way the Fox went, and when, and even why. The detective does another kind of trailing when he follows some trifling clue through the world of thought, tracing the secret of an unknown man along an invisible path, and running it to earth at last in the very heart that it belongs to.

The trailing of the Indian is these two combined. To a great extent his eyes do the work of the Hound's nose, but his own nose is not idle. When the trail disappears he must do the human detective work; but, under all circumstances, his brain must be backed by the finest senses, superb physique, and ripe experience, or he cannot hope to overmatch his prey.

From a hunter, perfectly equipped, one who knows the secrets of the trail, a Deer cannot escape. The trail may seem to end, but the trailer knows that it does not, except at the victim. It may elude him for a few hours, or even a day. It may puzzle him by side tracks and doubles, and may distance him by sheer speed, but it cannot shake him off. Sooner or later the tracker will run it down.

The trailer must know, first, his prey and its habits; second, its tracks and "sign"; and third, its other characteristics. Since the first requirement means a general knowledge of natural history, we must pass over that in this book, assuming that the trailer has it.

The trailer's next task is to learn the trails he means to follow. The Red Indian and the Bushman, of course, from the earliest days, simply memorize them; but *we* find it helpful and much easier to record them in some way. Aside from other considerations, a form is always better comprehended if we reproduce it visibly on paper.

As a general principle, no two kinds of animal leave the same track. As a matter of fact, no two individuals leave the same trail. Just as surely as there are differences of size and disposition, so will there be corresponding differences in the trail. But this is refining beyond the purposes of practicability in most cases; and, for the present, we may be satisfied to consider it a general rule that each species leaves its own clearly recognizable track.

One of my daily pastimes when the snow is on the ground is to take up some trail early in the morning, and follow it over hill and dale, carefully noting every change and every action as written in the snow. It is a wonderfully rewarding way of learning the methods and life of an animal. The trail records with perfect truthfulness everything that it did, or tried to do, at a time when it was unembarrassed by the nearness of its worst enemy. The trail is an autobiographical

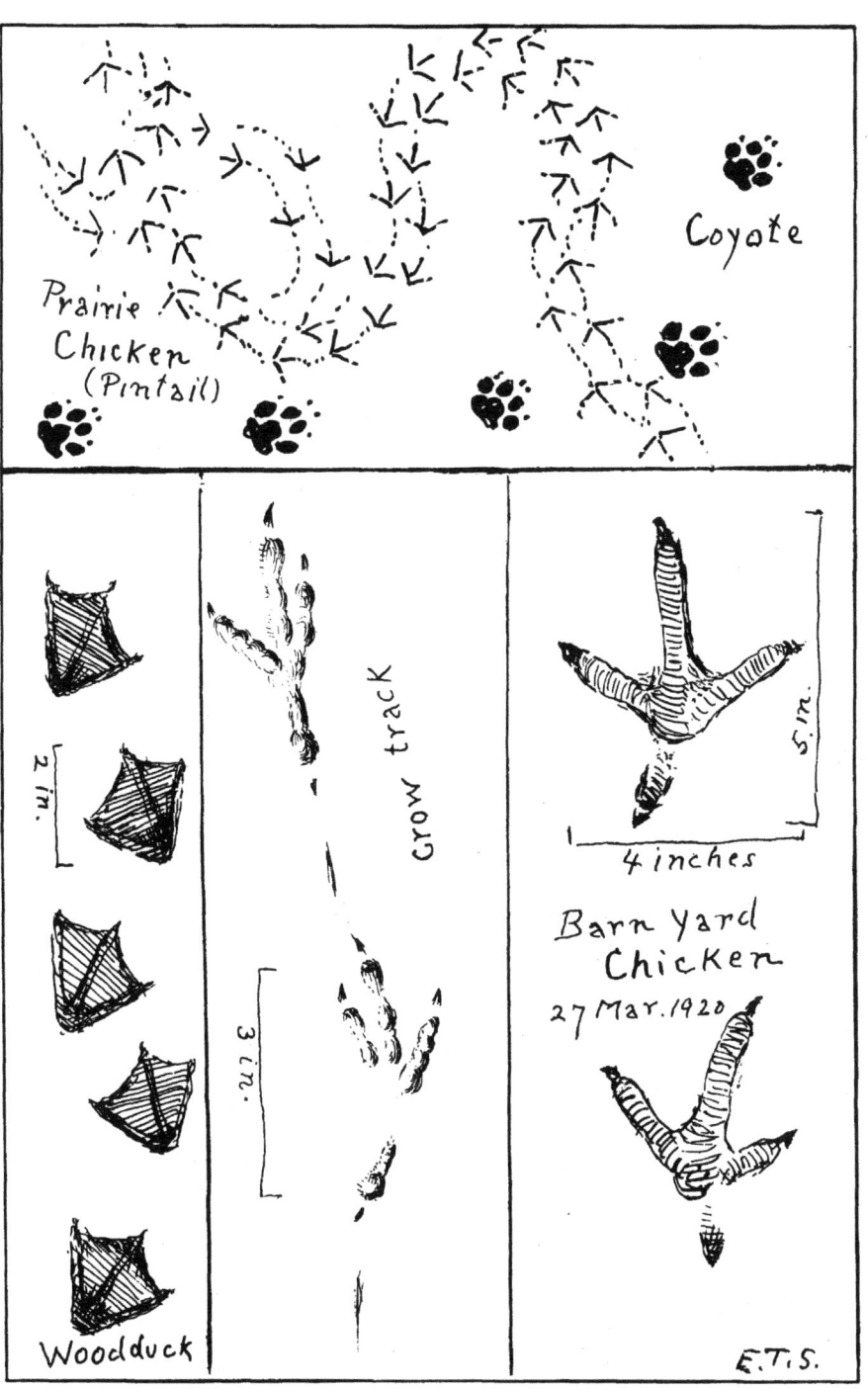

Birds on the ranch

chapter of the creature's life, written unwittingly indeed, and in perfect sincerity.

Whenever I find myself with time to pass at a railroad station in America, when there is snow on the ground, I endeavor to get out into the country. On such an occasion I rarely fail to find and read one of these more or less rewarding chapters, and thus get an insight into the local natural history of some animal.

But, as a rule, the first trails to catch the eye, and the best for first study, are those nearest home. Two well-marked types are the tracks of Cat and Dog (see page 70).

Most anatomists select the Cat as the ideal of muscle and bone structure; it is the perfect animal, and its track is also a good one to use for the standard.

On page 70 the roundness of the toe pads of the Cat track tell of their softness; their spread from each other shows the suppleness of the toes; the absence of claw marks tells of the retractability of their weapons. The front and hind feet are equal in length, but the front are broader. This is the rule among true quadrupeds.

The series of tracks, that is its "trail," shows the manner of the Cat *in walking*. In this, the animal used apparently but two legs, because the hind foot falls exactly on the track made by the front foot, each track being really doubled. This is perfect treading.

There are several advantages in this kind of walking. Every teamster knows that a wagon whose hind wheels do not exactly follow the front wheels is a very bad wagon to haul in sand, snow, or mud; the trail has to be broken twice, and the labor increased, some say, 50 per cent. This principle applies to the Cat track; by correct following, it goes more easily.

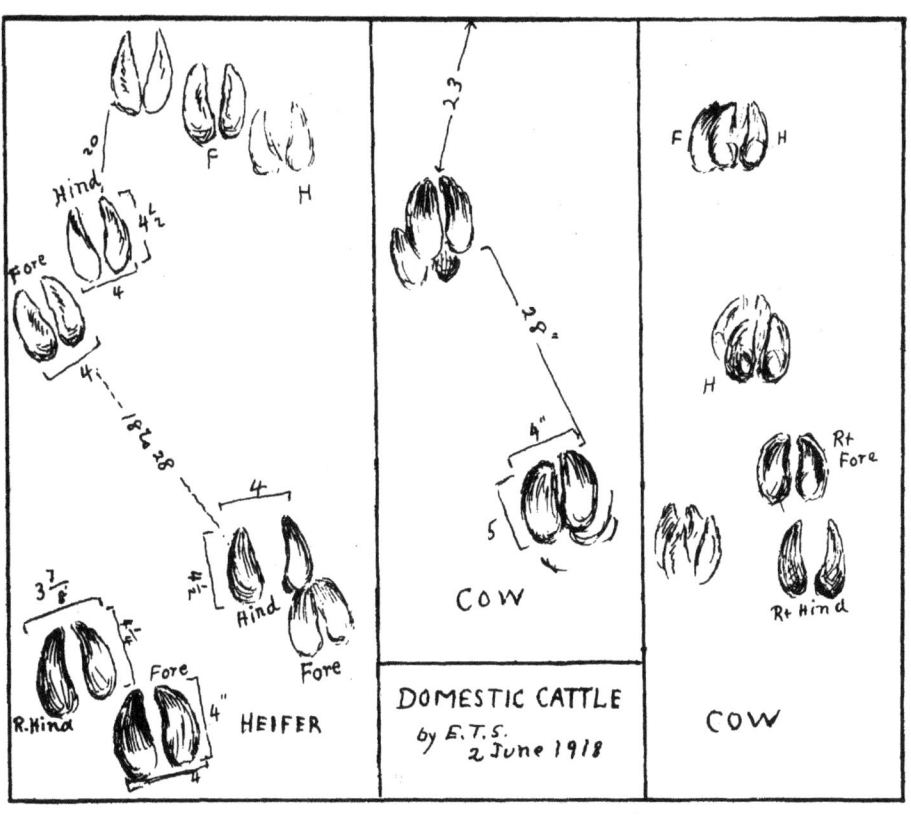

Tracks of domestic Cattle walking

But there is a still more important reason. A hunting Cat, sneaking through the woods after prey, must keep her eyes on the path ahead, or on the prey itself. At the very best, she may pick out a smooth, safe, silent place for the front feet to tread on. Especially at the climax of the hunt, all her senses are focused on the intended victim. She cannot select a safe spot for each hind foot in turn, even though the faintest crunch of a dry leaf will surely spoil the stalk. But there is no danger of that, for the Cat can see the spot selected for each front foot; and the hind feet are so perfectly trained that each seeks unerringly that very spot, the safe place that each front foot has just left. Thus, perfect stepping is silent stepping, and is essential to all creatures that stalk their prey.

The opposite kind of treading is seen in very heavy animals which frequent marshy ground; to them it would be a positive disadvantage to set the hind foot in the tread of the front foot when so much of the support has just been destroyed. Domestic Cattle illustrate this (page 55).

These principles are applicable to geology, where the trails are the only biographical records of certain species. From the manner of setting the feet we can distinguish the predacious and the marsh-frequenting quadrupeds.

In the track of the Dog the harder, less pliant foot and the non-retractile claws are clearly seen. But the trail shows that the ordinary Dog is not a correct stepper. His tracks are "out of register," as a printer would say. And usually he has a glaring defect, the result, no doubt, of domestication, of long generations on pavements and in houses—*he drags his toes.* All these things contribute to make the Dog a noisy walker in the woods.

It is well at this time to compare the track of the Dog

Dog and Wolf encounter at Buffalo Skull

with that of the Wolf. I have made dozens of drawings, casts, prints, photographs, and studies of Wolf and Dog tracks, and have not found a single reliable feature that will distinguish them.

One hunter says the Wolf has the relatively small outer toes. Yes, sometimes; but this is not so when compared with a Collie. Another says that the Wolf foot is longer; but it is not when compared with that of a Greyhound, Staghound, or Lurcher. Another declares that the Wolf's foot is larger; yet it will not rank in size with that of a Saint Bernard or a Great Dane. The Wolf lifts his feet nearly without dragging his toes; but so do many Dogs, especially country Dogs.

Thus, from time to time, all of these diagnostics fail. On the whole, a Wolf is a better walker than a Dog; his tracks do usually register, but not always, and in some Wolves rarely.

If a Wolf track in the snow be followed for a mile or two, it will be found to go cautiously up to any unusual or promising object; it is obviously the trail of a suspicious, shy creature. The Dog trail, on the other hand, is direct, and usually unafraid (see page 57).

However, this does not apply to the Dogs which poach or kill Sheep. There is, therefore, no sure means of distinguishing them, even in the wilderness. One can judge only by probabilities. I have often heard inexperienced hunters boast that they could "tell them every time," but old hunters usually say, "No man can tell for sure."

7 *A Rabbit Adventure*

America is well provided with Rabbits and Hares. A score or more of species are now recognized. Two very well-known types are the Cottontail of the woods and the Jack Rabbit of the plains.

The Cottontail is much like an English Rabbit; but it is a little smaller, has shorter ears, the whole underpart of the tail is glorified into a fluffy, snowy powder puff. It leads the life of a Hare, not usually making burrows, but entering burrows at times under the stress of danger. As the Cottontail bounds, the hind feet track ahead of the front feet; and the faster the Rabbit goes, the farther ahead its hind feet get. This is true of all quadrupeds that bound, but is more apparent in the Rabbit, because the fore and hind feet differ so much in size.

The Jack Rabbit of Kansas is the best known of the long-eared Jacks. The greater size of the marks and the double lengths of the bounds are the obvious, but not important differences; because a *young* Jack would come down to the Cottontail standard.

I have found two reliable differences. First, the Jack's feet are rarely paired when he is bounding at full speed. The Cottontail pairs his hind feet, but not his front. Animals that climb usually pair their front feet in running, just as tree birds hop when on the ground. Second, the stroke (x) that is shown on pages 61 and 65 is diagnostic of the southern Jack Rabbit; it is the mark made by the long hanging tail.

Each of the four types of Hare common in the temperate parts of America has its own style of tail and fashion of wearing it (page 63).

The Northern or White-tailed Jack has his tail pure white, and he carries it straight out level.

The Southern or Black-tailed Jack has his tail jet black on the upper part, and he carries it straight down.

The Varying Hare, or White Rabbit, has an inconsequent little upturned tuft like a tear in his brown pantaloons, showing the white undergarment.

The Cottontail has his latter end brown above, but he keeps it curled up tight on his back so as to show nothing but the gleaming white puff of cotton on a helpful background of rich brown.

The tails of the Cottontail and the Varying Hare never touch the ground except when their owners sit down on them.

The most specialized features of any animal are always its most variable features. The Jack Rabbit's tailpiece is much subject to variation; and the long, deep intertrackial dash that it makes in the snow is a better guide to the in-

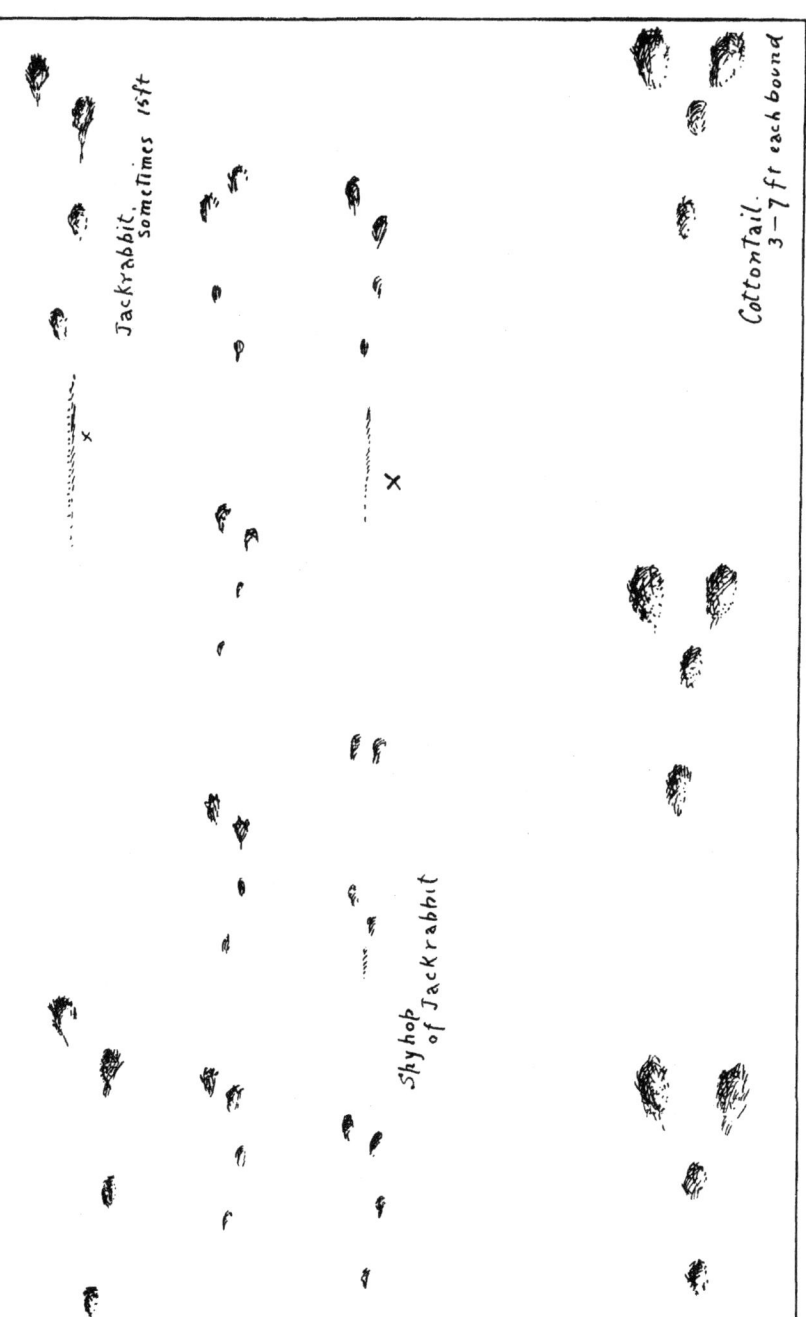

Jack Rabbit leaves a tail mark as he runs; Cottontail leaves no tail mark

ANIMAL TRACKS AND HUNTER SIGNS

dividual that made it than would be the tracks of all four feet together.

During February 1902 at Newton, Kansas, I found myself with a day to spare. At the hotel office I asked the usual question: "Any wild animals about here?" and got the usual answer: "No, all been shot off."

I walked down the street four blocks from the hotel and found a Jack Rabbit trail in the snow. A little farther on I found some Cottontail tracks, though still in town. I walked a mile into the country and met an old farmer who said that "no Rabbits are ever found around here."

A quarter of a mile away was an orchard; and, beside it, a fence half buried in snowdrifts that were yellowed with tall dead grass sticking through. This was promising, so I went there, and on the edge of the drift found a Jack Rabbit form or den, with fresh tracks leading out and away at full speed. There were no tracks leading in; so he must have gone in there before the last snow came, and that was the night before.

When a Jack runs without fear of any enemy at hand, he goes much like a Fox or an Antelope; but when an enemy is close, he runs with long, low hops, six or seven in succession, then gives an upright leap or "spy-hop" to take an observation (see page 65).

A silly young Jack will lose time by taking one hop in three for observation; but a very clever old fellow is content with one in ten. Here, then, was the trail of this Jack straight away, but taking about one observation in twelve hops.

I followed, and found he had made for a fence a quarter mile off, and there had sat for some time observing; had then taken alarm and run toward a farmyard, a quarter

Rabbit labels

mile farther on, taking occasional observation hops. At the barnyard fence he had sat for a time, then followed his back track to the main road, where possibly he had hoped to hide his trail. Down this he had gone, taking *no* observations.

A Dog was lying on a doorstep by the road; and past this Dog he had taken twenty-foot leaps. Two hundred yards down this highway he had turned abruptly, as though a man coming in sight had scared him. I now began to think the Jack was near me, although so far I had not seen him.

The trail led on through several barbwire fences and some hedges, then made for another barnyard, and showed that the animal had taken some observations which had resulted in his doubling his speed. The barnyard was possessed of a Cat, and there was a dangerous-looking Dog in it; so I went around and found the Rabbit track on the other side. He passed under several bad fences and made for another barnyard half a mile off.

I was now satisfied that he was only a little ahead of me, so I ceased watching the track so closely, scanning rather the open plain ahead. Then, farther on, under a barbwire fence, sitting up watching me, at last I saw my Jack. He hopped away at once, making a high jump often to look around.

He never let me get within two hundred yards, and he wasted but little time in observation. He had now taken me on a two-mile circuit and brought me back to the starting point. Thus, he had taught me this: a cunning old Jack Rabbit lived in the region around which I had followed him—for they keep to their home grounds. All his ways of running and observing, and of using barbwire fences, barnyards, and hedges, showed that he was very clever; but the best proof of that was in the fact that he could live and

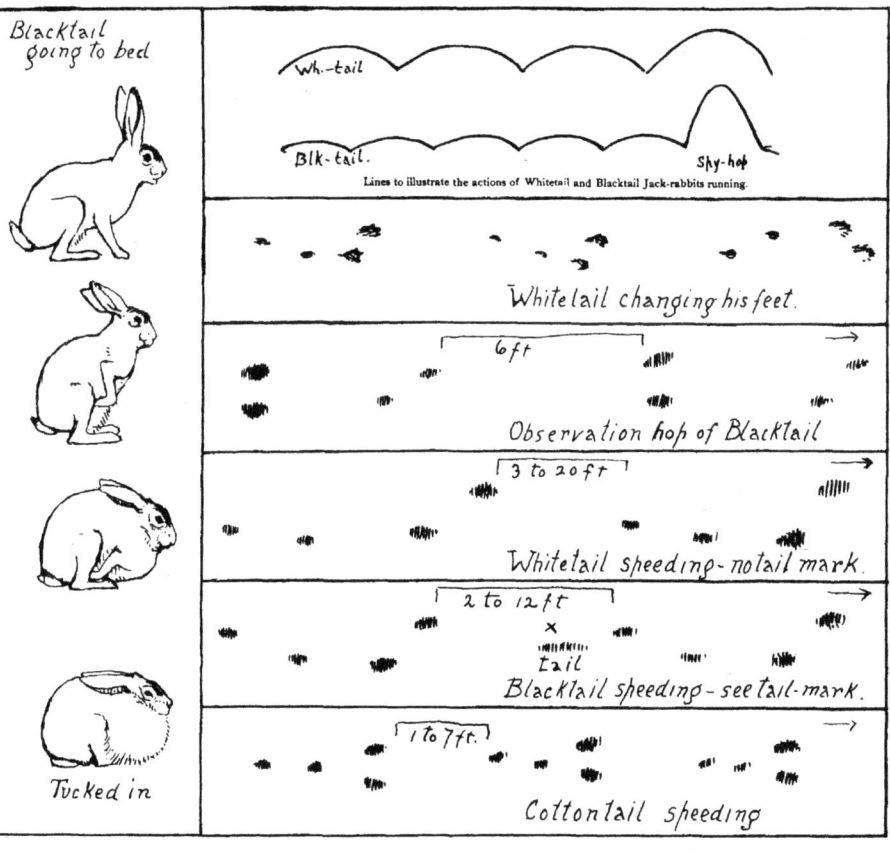

Tracks of Rabbits

flourish on the edge of a town that was swarming with Dogs, and traveled over daily by men with guns.

The next day I had another opportunity of going to the Jack Rabbit's home region. I did not see him, but I saw his fresh tracks; then later I saw where these had joined on to the fresh tracks of another Rabbit. I sketched all the salient points and noted that now my big Jack had followed the other. They had dodged about here and there, and then one had overtaken the other. Here they frolicked together in the friendliest fashion (opposite page).

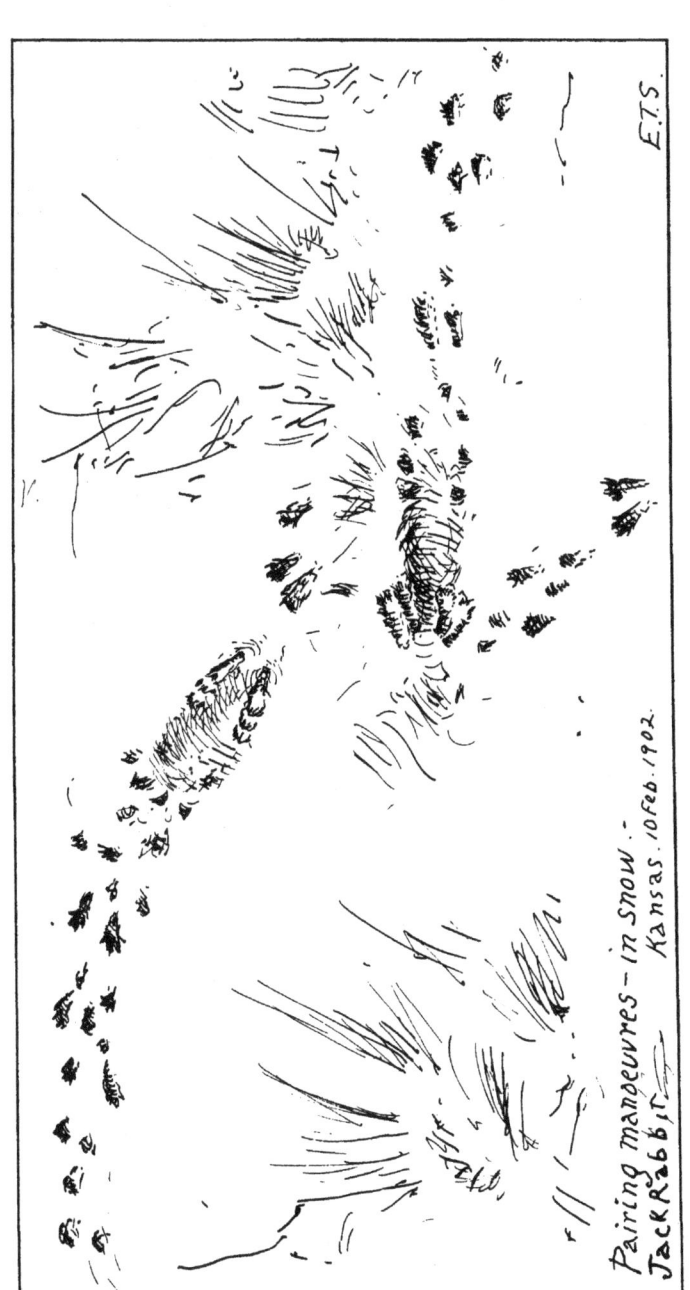

Jack Rabbits frolicking

8   Around an Eastern Farm

To learn tracking, it is well to begin with tracks that all can find and identify with certainty. Naturally, then, we take first the friendly familiar Dog and Cat; and, because near at hand, we should add to this the track of the common Red Fox of the northeastern states.

The best identification of a track is watching the animal while he is making it. It is well, also, to draw all tracks of natural size when possible, and give one of the front feet and one of the hind, because they differ. Remember, further, that the trail, i.e., the long series of tracks, is just as important as the single track, but naturally, can seldom be given life-size.

In all cases it is important to indicate the scale. On page 70 we have the tracks of Dog, Fox, and Cat for comparison. One of the first things to note is that no claws show in the Cat's trail, although she has the best claws of the three. Her claws, however, are too good to waste on the mud, so she pulls them in; thus, they are kept sharp for service.

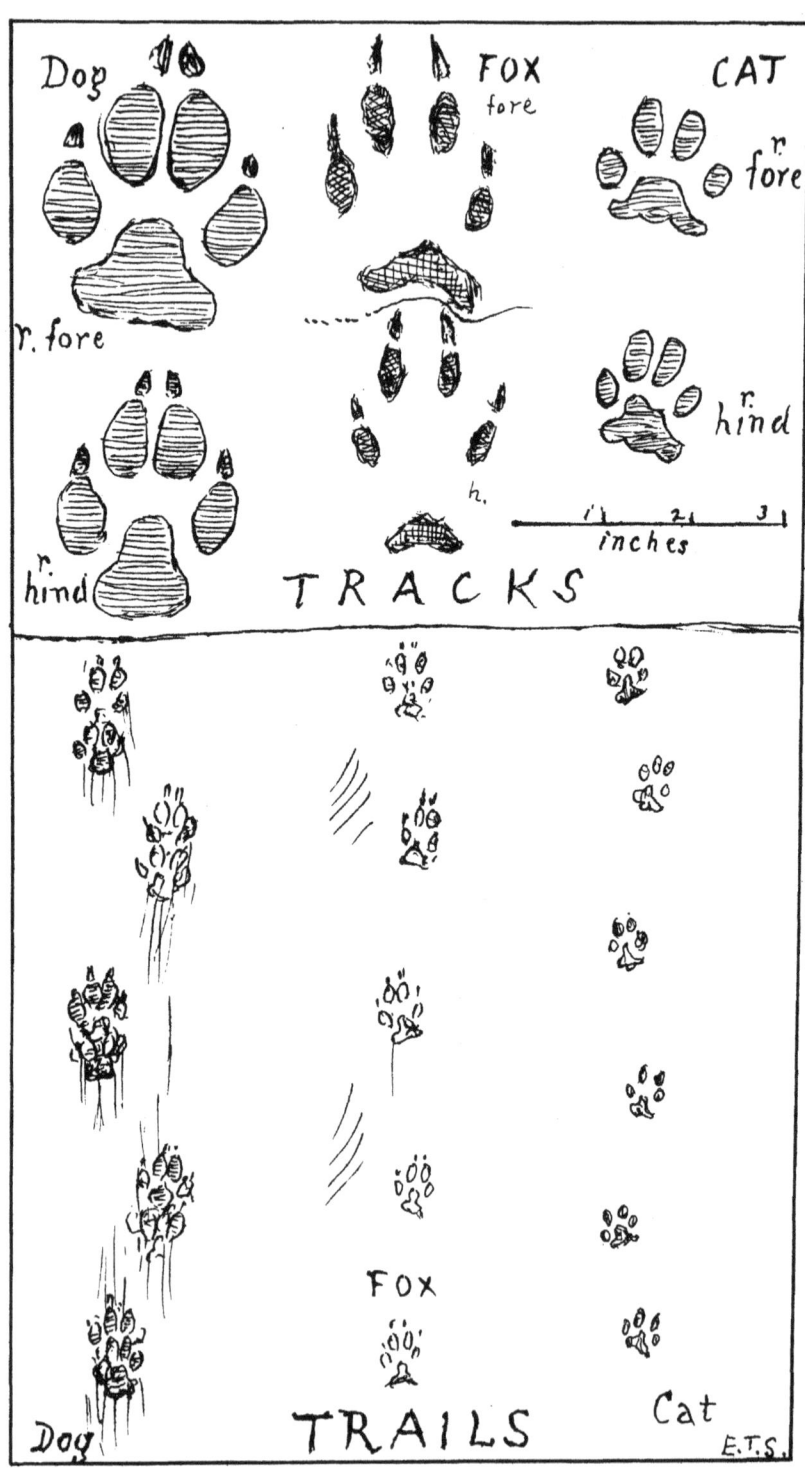

Trails of a Dog, Fox, and Cat

Note, next, that the back edge of the Cat's heel pad is indented; as is also that of the Fox. All of the Cat family have more or less of this indentation. If you turn to the blacktrack of the Texan Lynx on page 49, you will see it at its greatest development.

The trail of the Dog shows two curious features not seen in the other two: first, the incorrect register of front and hind feet; and, second, the dragging of the toes. These characteristics have been already discussed in Chapter 6.

A diagnostic of the Fox track is the soft brush mark on the snow at one side—the downwind side (page 95). This is made by the big blowsy tail of the Fox, driven by the wind, so it touches the snow and leaves the telltale trace. This mark is not usually seen on the trails of Dog or Cat, for more or less obvious reasons.

9 Marsh and Woodland Creatures

Every old farmhouse in New England, indeed in the whole eastern States and Canada, has in its near neighborhood a brook, a pond, a little woodland, and more or less of a marsh or swamp. Thus, the human inhabitants are brought in contact with a new order of wild things not naturally included in the list of creatures that dwell in orchard, uplands, or level fields under crop.

The new list of fourfoots is not only different and long. It is more primitive in its membership; for the swamp, the marsh, and the untillable wilds have always been the safe refuge of the creatures that are unhappy with man too near. These are really the aboriginal population.

All my life I have sought after and loved the marshes. The great marsh near Toronto was one of the precious places and Edenlands of my boyhood. It taught me the glory, the sanctity, the final haven value of the swamplands; and out of a lifetime of joyful experience I invite our young people to come marsh-wading with me, and learn the actuality of the Paradise that a marsh fails never to create.

The advantages of the marsh are many. It has food, water, and shelter. It is never disturbed by the plow, and rarely by men during the summertime. It has usually a fringe of trees which completes its variation of cover, all of which things combine to make the marsh an ideal natural sanctuary.

I have seen one or two marshes destroyed by drainage or filling, and in each case the neighborhood lamented the loss. It had been a retreat of wildlife, harmless and delightful; now it was gone, without any compensating advantage.

The muddy margins and open flats of the marsh afford wonderful visitors' albums for the wild things to inscribe their names, with or without some sentiment suggested by the experience of the occasion.

As samples of these inscriptions, see pages 75 and 76.

It would be easy to add a long chapter on the signs and signals of birds, also their recognition marks. But I have already treated the subject at length in my autobiography,* as well as in numerous articles that appeared in *The Auk*.

Trail of an Artist-Naturalist, published by Scribner in 1940.

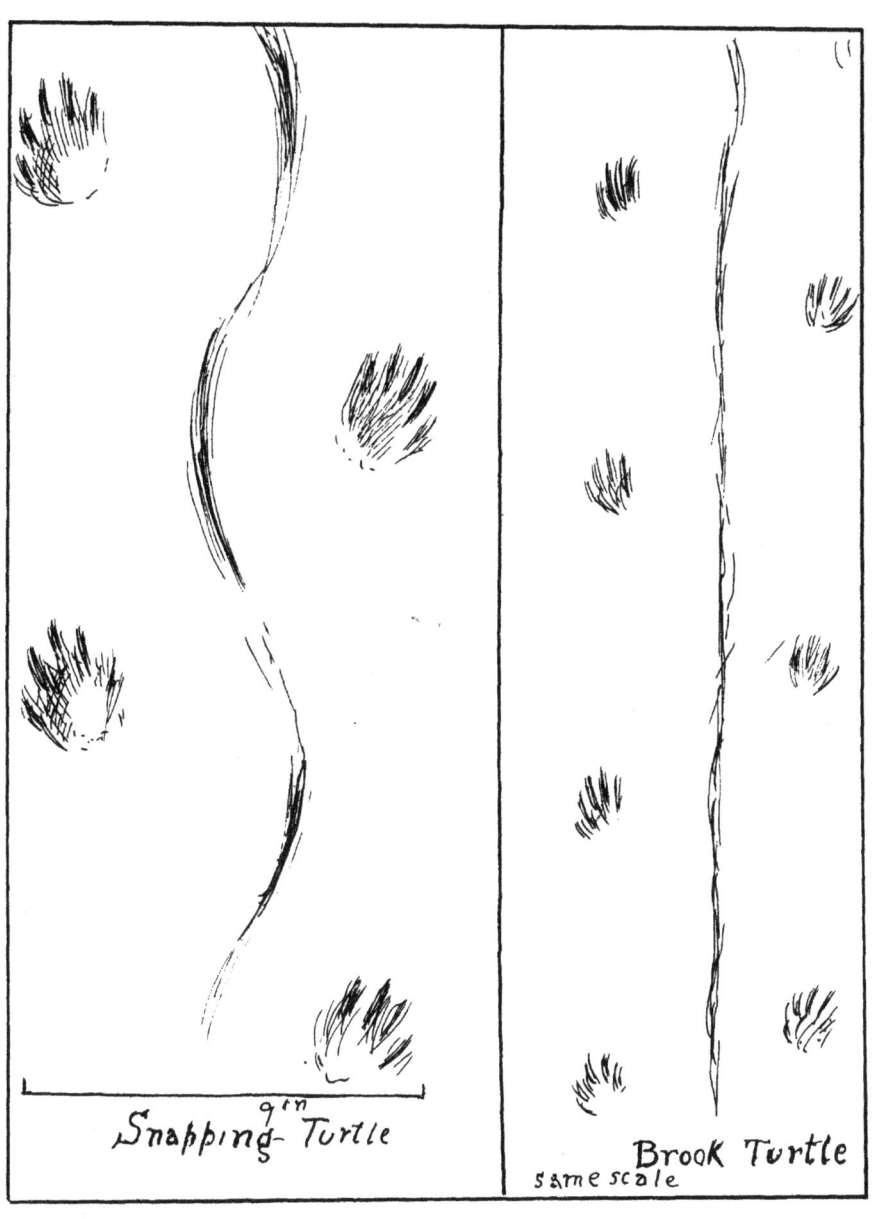

Turtle tracks in mud

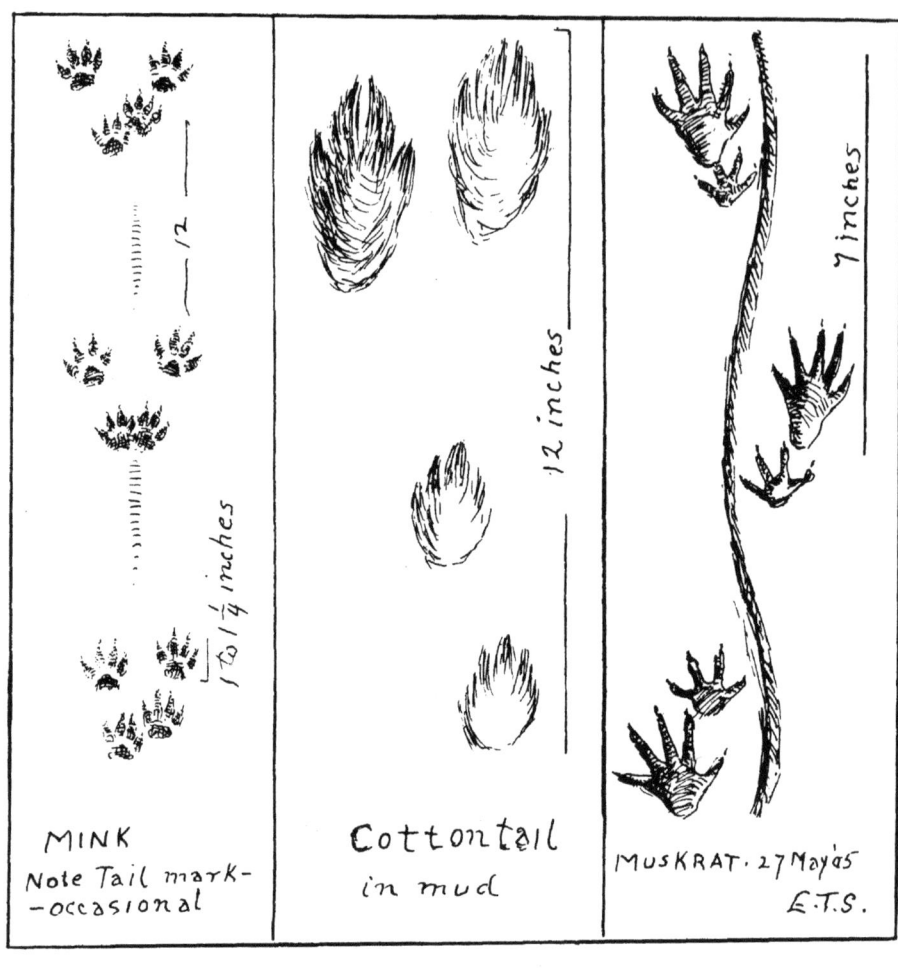

Tracks in the mud

10 Track History of Mink and Rabbit

It was in the winter of 1900. I was standing with my brother, a businessman, on Goat Island, Niagara, when he remarked: "How is it, you and I have been in the same parts of America for twenty years; yet I never see any of the curious sides of animal life that you are continually discovering?"

"Largely because you do not study tracks," was my reply. "Look at the snow by your feet now. There is a whole history to be read."

"I see some marks," he replied, "that might have been made by an animal."

"That is the track of a Cottontail," I answered. "The snow is too deep and powdery to record all the details of anatomy; but the size and the general features make the species unmistakable. Now let us read this chapter of his life." (Page 79.)

"See, he was going toward the West. I know this because the larger marks (made by the hind feet) are ahead of the small marks (made by the fore feet), as is the case with all fourfoots which bound when speeding. He went in a general straight course, as though making for some well-known haunt. His easy pace, with eight or ten inches between each set of tracks, shows unalarm. But see here, joining on, is something else."

"So there is! Another Cottontail."

"Not at all. This new track is smaller, the fore feet are more or less paired, showing that this creature can climb a tree. There is a suggestion of toe pads, and there is a mark telling evidently of a long tail, low held. These things, combined with the size, the spacing, and the place, indicate clearly the trail of a Mink.

"See! He also saw the Rabbit track; and finding it fresh-smelling, he followed it. His bounds are lengthened now; but the Rabbit's are not, showing that the latter was unconscious of the pursuit."

We followed, and after a hundred yards, the double trail led us to a great pile of wood. Into this both tracks went.

"Still following the Rabbit," I explained, "the Mink has tracked him into his hiding place under the timber pile. Now we shall go around the pile to make sure that neither of them went out."

We did so, and found no tracks whatever. Therefore, I was justified in continuing: "Now, brother, if you will take the trouble to remove all these sticks and logs, I will guarantee that in the middle of it, you will find, first, the remains of the Rabbit, partly devoured; and then, nearby, the Mink curled up asleep after his feast."

As the pile was large and the conclusion more or less self-evident, my brother was content to accept my reading of the episode.

Neither of us had any doubt as to the truth of the story I told—yet neither of us had at any time had a single glimpse of either Rabbit or Mink.

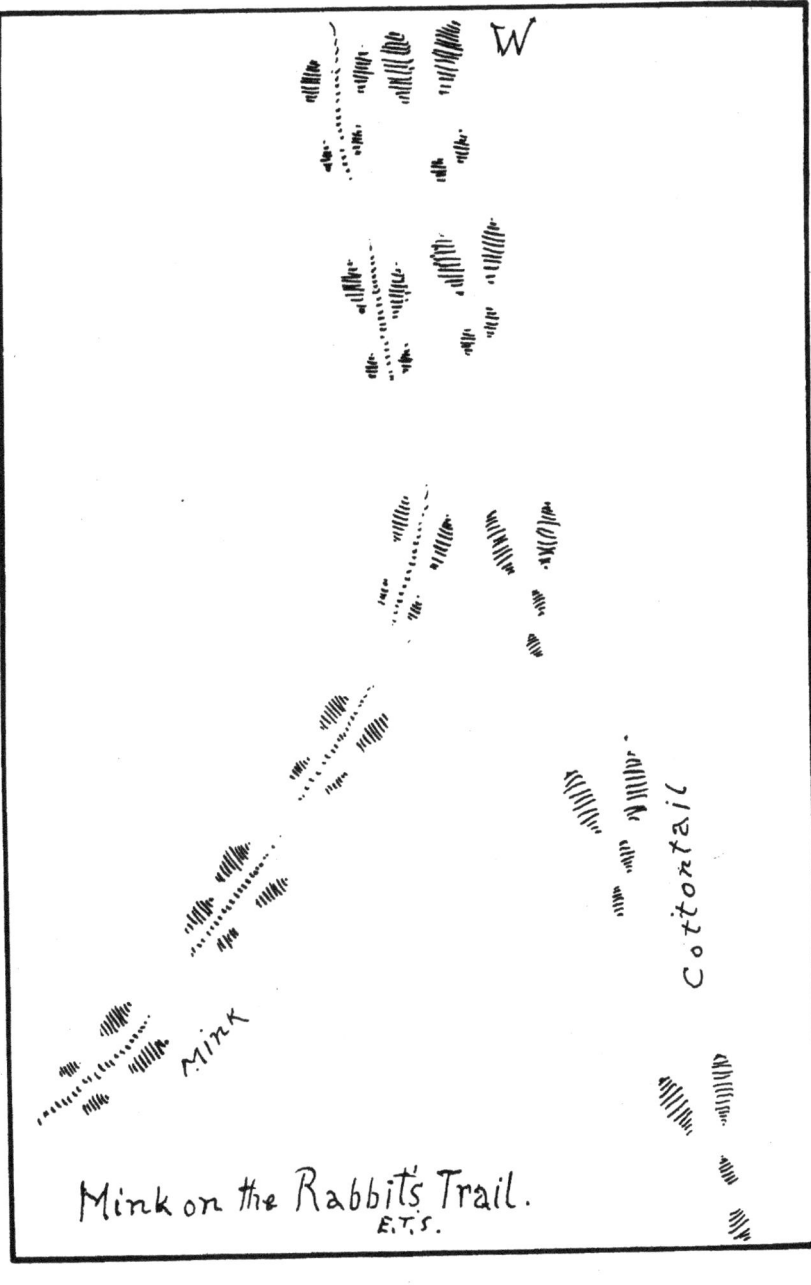

11 Record of a Woodland Tragedy

On February 15, 1885, near Toronto, I made the record shown on page 83. It is really a condensation of the facts, as the trail is shortened where uninteresting.

At A, I found a round place about five inches by nine, where a Cottontail had crouched during the light snowfall. At B, he had leaped out and sat looking around. The small prints in front were made by his fore feet, the two long ones by his hind feet; and farther back is a little dimple made by the tail, showing that he was sitting on it.

Something apparently alarmed him, causing him to dart out at full speed toward C and D. Now a remarkable change is to be seen. The marks made by the front feet are behind the large marks made by the hind feet, because the Rabbit overreaches each time, the hind feet track ahead of the front feet. The faster he goes, the farther ahead those hind feet get; and what would happen if he multiplied his speed by ten, I really cannot imagine. This overreach of the hind feet takes place in most bounding animals.

Now the Cottontail began a series of the most extraordinary leaps and dodgings (D,E,F) as though trying to escape from some enemy. But what enemy? There were no other tracks. I began to think the Rabbit was crazy, was flying from an imaginary foe, that possibly I was on the trail of a March Hare.

But at G, I found, for the first time, some spots of blood. This told me that the Rabbit was in real danger, but it gave no clue as to the source of that danger. A few yards farther, at H, I found more blood. Twenty yards more, at I, on each side of the Rabbit trail were the obvious marks of a pair of broad, strong wings.

Oho! Now I knew the mystery of the Cottontail running from a foe that left no track. He was pursued by an eagle, a hawk, or an owl.

A few yards more and I found the remains (J) of the Cottontail partly devoured. This put the eagle out of the question; an eagle would have carried the Rabbit off bodily. A hawk or an owl, then, was the assassin.

I looked for something to decide which, and, close by the remains, found the peculiar two-paired track of an owl. A hawk's track would have been as at K, three toes forward and one toe back; while the owl nearly always sets its feet on the ground with two toes back.

But which owl? There were in the valley at least three species that might be blamed. I looked for more proof, and got it on a nearby sapling—one small feather (L), downy, as are all owl feathers, and bearing three broad bars; telling me plainly that a barred owl had been there lately, and that, therefore, he was almost certainly the slayer of the Cottontail.

As I busied myself making notes, what should come flying

A woodland tragedy

up the valley but the owl himself, back to the very place of the crime, no doubt intent on completing his meal. He alighted on a branch ten feet above my head, just over the Rabbit remains, and sat there muttering in his throat. I had neither gun nor camera, but he remained very still for a long time. A sketchbook was at hand, so I made a portrait, which is now among my trophies of the chase.

The proof in this case was purely circumstantial; but I think that we can come to only one conclusion—that the evidence of the track in the snow was complete and convincing.

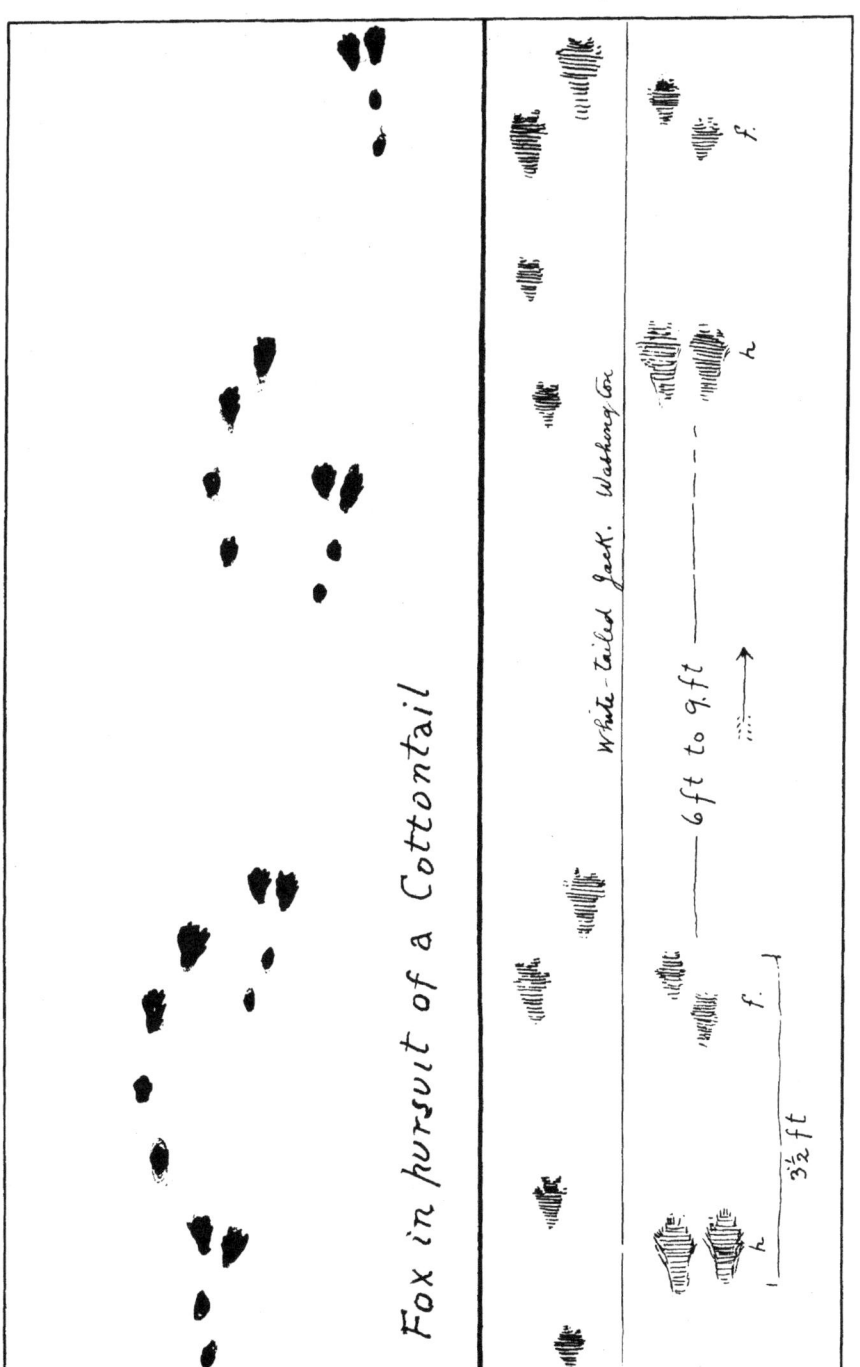

Rabbits and Fox speeding

12 Out West

My homeland near Santa Fe has great stretches of pine forest, varied with beautiful little prairies, and a background of rugged granite peaks, the southmost extension of the Rocky Mountains. There is every type of environment except swamps and lakes. Water is scarce, but there is enough for dry-land creatures; and the result is a profusion of wildlife of all kinds but fish.

Birds and mammals abound. Soon, however, the young naturalist realizes that, with a few exceptions in each case, birds are creatures of sunlight and are rarely seen at night; whereas mammals are creatures of the night and are seldom seen by day.

Coyotes are plentiful in this region; we hear their weird music every night. Yet we do not see a dozen Coyotes in the course of a year, and might be without proof of their existence but for the ever-present, never-failing hunter sign—the tracks of the animals in the dust, in the mud, in the snow.

There was a time when the Gray Wolf, Buffalo Wolf or

Lobo, also abounded; but these, alas! have disappeared from most of the Cattle country, owing to the continual hunting, trapping, and poisoning to which they have been subjected by the cattlemen.

On page 89 is a drawing I made to illustrate the tracks, the distant silhouette, and the contrasting details of Wolf, Coyote, and Fox.

The Wolf track differs from that of the usual type of Dog chiefly in size, but the Coyote presents a characteristic that I long ago observed, though never yet have fully explained.

In most animals the two central toe pads of the fore feet are much larger than those at each side. (For illustration compare Gray Wolf and Fox in the plate.) In the Coyote track, however, as shown in the plate, the two outer pads are markedly larger than the two inner or central toe pads. This I have found to be the rule in the tracks of this animal, and yet I can find nothing in the anatomy of the animal to correspond with or justify the difference in size. I have had to accept it, unexplained. However, my knowledge stood me in good stead on one occasion.

In my younger days I had been plugging along as a naturalist of the usual type, trying merely to accumulate specimens and facts. Then I began to convey my facts in the form of romantic stories—fiction in form of presentation, but solid fact in their basis and their message. These grew in popularity through the '80s, but had their climax in the '90s. In 1898, my book, *Wild Animals I Have Known*, reached the peak of being a best seller.

This was most satisfactory to me and made me hosts of friends; but it also made me many enemies among the older school of naturalists, whose works, though sincere and truthful, had brought but poor returns from the people at large.

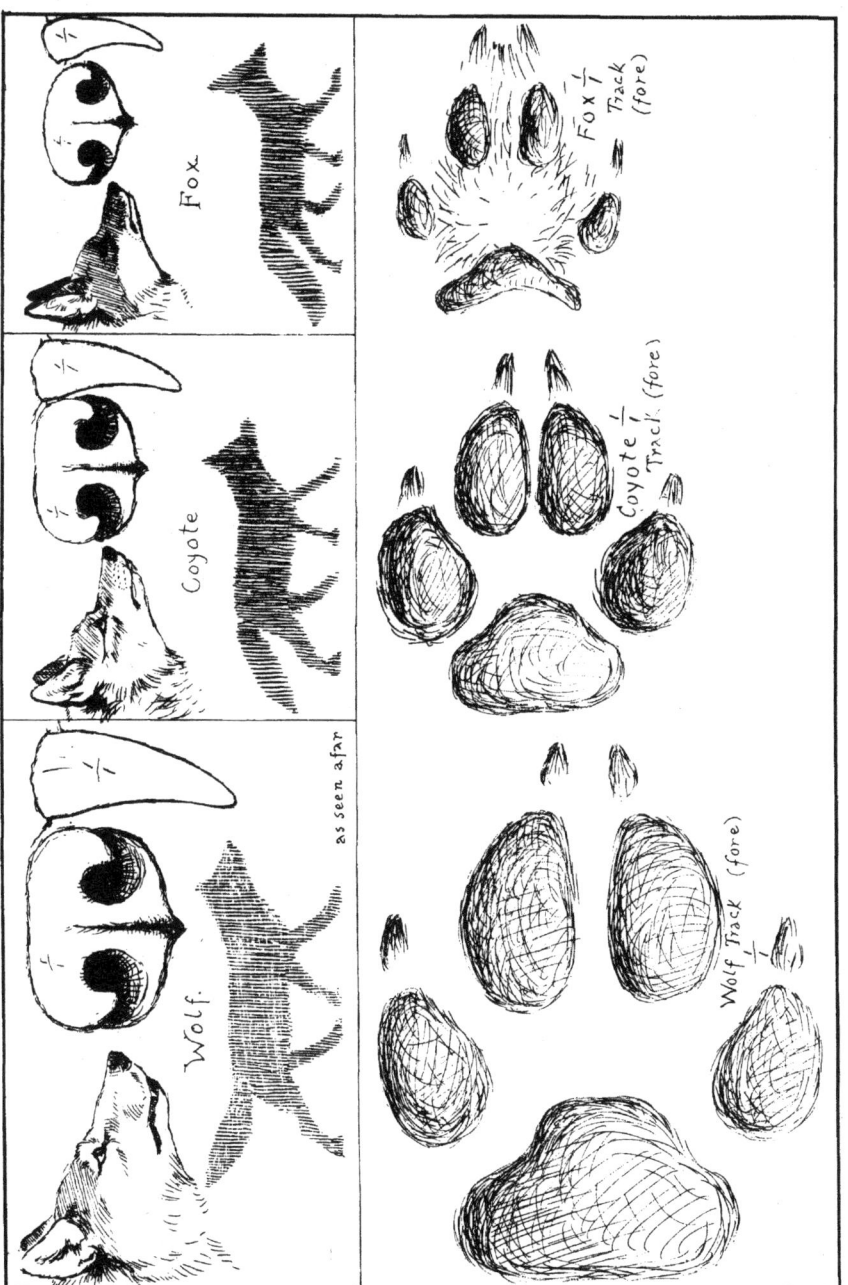

Characteristics of Wolf, Coyote, and Fox. Snout, upper canine and track

Their attitude to me was jealous and hostile.

John Muir was well known as a good naturalist, described as "The Grand Old Man of the Sierras." He had paid no attention to my work when, in the autumn of 1899, I visited California. Prominent men and publishers showed me much honor, and my friends were determined that I should meet John Muir. Accordingly, on October 2, 1899, I was taken to Muir's home in the little town of Martinez, not far from San Francisco.

I found the venerable old gentleman coldly aloof and little disposed to converse. All his remarks referred to his own discoveries among the glaciers. Evidently he did not accept me as a naturalist.

However, he showed me his garden with pride. As we examined and admired his watermelons, we came on one partly devoured; and as I stooped to study the track of the depredator, I exclaimed: "Well, if I saw that out in the wilderness, I should call it a Coyote track."

"Huh!" he grunted, "that's just what it is. I can't keep the brutes from sneaking in by night and mangling my watermelons. But how do *you* know it's a Coyote?"

"See there," I said. "At first sight, it is the track of a middle-sized Dog, but the two outer toe pads are bigger then the two inner ones. That is the mark of the Coyote."

"I give in!" he declared. "Now I know you are a naturalist."

From that time on he was most genial, and accepted me as one of the real brotherhood.

On page 57, we get a little glimpse into the contrasted mentality of Dog and Wolf, and this generalization would hold also with Fox or Coyote as well as Wolf.

In the old days, there were many Buffalo skulls scattered

over the Plains. These always offered the possibility of food, or at least they were used by the canine animals as places of uric record. Therefore, all Dogs, Wolves, and Coyotes made a point of calling at them. However, most of the wild creatures, if old and experienced, knew that there was also a possibility there of traps and poison baits. So they made their approach with due caution—up the wind; and then executed a careful back-off on finding nothing of value. This method is illustrated on the plate in the trail of the Wolf.

The Dog, on the other hand, little used to traps or poison, goes splashing and blundering straight up to the Buffalo skull, just as do our town Dogs to a lamppost; there leaves his uric record for those whom it may concern, and goes straight away again when he finds it has nothing of interest for him.

13 A Chapter of Fox Life

One day in Manitoba, soon after the snow had come, I set out on one of my long decipherments. The day before, I had followed a Fox trail for three or four miles, to learn only that he tacked upwind and smelled at every log, bump, and tree that stuck through the snow; that he had followed a White Hare at full speed, but was easily left behind when the Hare got into its ancient stronghold, the scrubby, brushy woods.

This morning I took up another Fox trail (page 95). The frost was intense, the snow was dry and powdery. As each foot of the Fox had been raised, the white dust had fallen back into the track, so that the mark was merely a shapeless dimple in the whiteness. No telltale evidences of toes and claws were there, but still I knew it for a Fox trail. How? It was too small for a Coyote, so that there were but two others in that region that might have been confounded with it: one, a very large House Cat; the other, a very small House Dog.

The Fox has the supple paw of the Cat; it spreads even

more, *but it shows the long, intractile claws.* As a stepper, the Fox ranks close to the Cat. His trail is noted also for its narrowness; that is, the feet are set nearly in one straight line. This in a trail usually means a swift animal; whereas the widely spread marks, seen at a maximum in the Badger, indicate a broad chest, and great but sluggish strength.

The remoteness from the house put the Cat out of the reckoning. Besides, at one or two places the paw had grazed the snow, showing two long furrows—the marks of claws that do not sheath. The tracks were aligned like a Cat's, but were fourteen inches apart, while it is rare for a Cat to step more than ten.

A Dog's marks, perhaps, but never a Cat's.

However, I soon decided against their being the tracks of a Dog. First, the probabilities were against it; second, the marks were nearly in a line, showing a chest too narrow for a Dog. Also, the toes did not drag, though there was four inches of snow. The register could not be distinguished.

But there was one feature that settled all doubt—the big, soft, blowsy, shallow marks of the Fox's brush (x x page 95), sometimes sweeping the snow at every yard, sometimes not at all for fifty steps; but telling me with certainty (founded in part on the other things) that this was the trail of a Fox.

Which way is he going? was the next question. Not easy to say when the toe tracks do not show. This was settled by the faint claw marks already noted. If still in doubt, I could follow till the Fox chanced on some place under a thick tree, or on ice where there was very little snow, and here a distinct impression might be found.

I have often seen a curiously clear track across ice, made by a gentle breeze blowing away all the snow except that

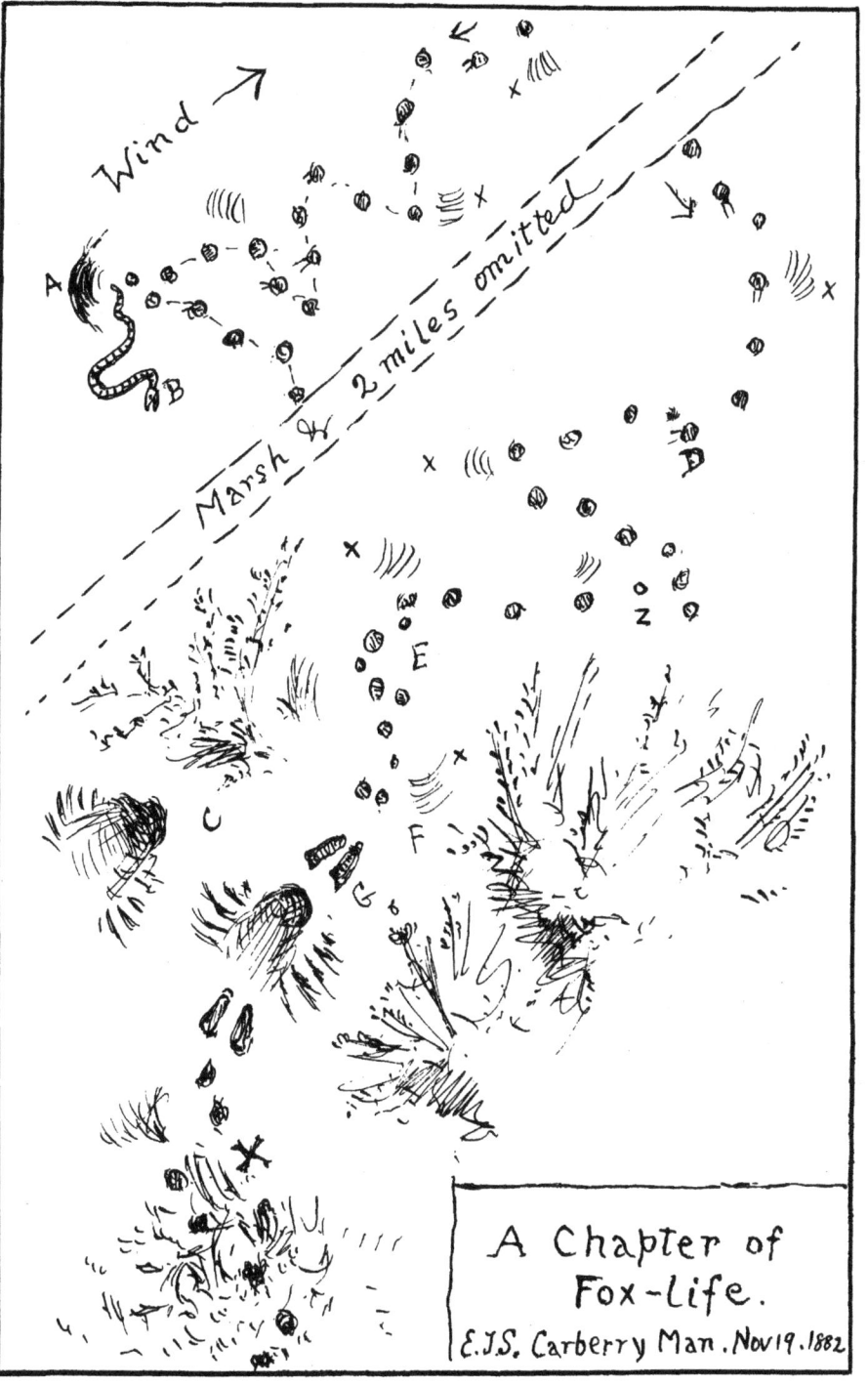

pressed down hard by the impact of the toes, so that the black ice underneath has a row of clear-cut raised white tracks, a line of Fox-track cameos, cut sharp on a black ice base.

For a mile or two I followed my Fox. Nothing happened. I got only the thought that his life was largely made up of nose investigation and unfavorable reports from the committee in charge.

Then I came to a long, sloping hollow. The Fox trotted down this; and near its lower end he evidently got a nose report of importance, for he had swung to the right and gone slowly—so said the short steps—zigzagging up the wind. Within fifteen feet the tracks in the course shortened from four or five feet to nothing, and ended in a small hole in a bank (A).

From this the Fox had pulled out a common, harmless garter snake, torpid, and doubtless curled up there to sleep away the winter. The Fox chopped the snake across the spine with his powerful meat cutters, killed it, dropped it on the snow (B); then, without eating a morsel of it as far as I could see, went on with his hunt.

Why he should kill a creature that he did not eat, I could not understand. I thought that ferocious sort of vice was limited to mankind; but clearly the Fox was guilty of the human crime, for there lay the dead snake on the trail.

The dotted guide led me now with numerous halts and devious turns, across a great marsh that had doubtless furnished many a fattened Mouse in other days, but now the snow and ice made such a hunt fruitless.

Farther on, the country was open in places, with clumps of timber; and into this, from the wide marsh, had blown a great bank of soft and drifted snow.

A CHAPTER OF FOX LIFE

Manitoban winters are not noted for their smiling geniality or profusion of outdoor flowers. Frost and snow are sure to come early and continue till spring. The thermometer may be for weeks about zero point. It may, on occasion, dip down until it reaches thirty, or even forty, degrees below; and, whenever, with that cold, there also comes a gale of wind, it conjures up the awful tempest of the snow, the blizzard.

The blizzard is a terror to wildlife out on the plains. When it comes, the biggest, strongest, and best clad rush for shelter. They know that to face it means death.

The prairie chickens or grouse have learned the lesson of the blizzard long ago. What shelter can they seek? There is only one—an Eskimo shelter, a snowhouse. They can hide in a protecting drift of snow.

As the night comes then, with the fearful frost and driving clouds of white, the chickens seek a snowdrift; not on the open plain, for there the snow is hammered hard by the wind; but on the edge of the woods, where tall grass spears or scattering twigs stick up through, and keep the snow from packing. Deep into this the chickens dive, each making a place for itself (C).

The wind soon wipes out all traces, levels off each hole, and hides them well. There they remain till the morning, warm and safe. Unless—and here is the chief danger—some wild animal comes by during the night, scents them, finds them in there, and seizes them before they can escape.

This chapter of grouse history was doubtless an old story to the Fox that I was trailing; and coming near the woodland edge, his shortened steps showed that he knew it for a land of promise.

At D he came to a sudden stop. Some wireless message on

the wind had warned him of game at hand. He paused here with foot upraised. I knew it, for I found his record of the act (Z). The little mark there was not a full track, but the paw's tip print, showing that the Fox had not set the foot down, but held it poised in a Pointer Dog pose, as his nose was harkening to the telltale wind.

Then from D to E he went slowly. I knew it was slowly, because the steps were so short. Now he paused; the promising scent was lost. He stood in doubt (so said the telltale snow, in the only universal tongue). Then the hunter turned and slowly worked on, while frequent broad touches in the snow (x x x) continued the guarantee that the maker of these tracks was neither docked nor spindle-tailed.

From E to F the shortened steps with frequent marks of pause and pose showed how the scent was warming—how well the Fox knew some good thing was near.

At F he stood still for some time, with both feet set down in the snow. So it was written. This was the critical moment. And straight up the redolent wind he went, following his nose, cautiously and silently as possible, realizing that now a single heedless step might spoil the hunt.

At G were the deeply imprinted marks of both hind feet, showing where the Fox had sprung just at the split second when, from the spotless snowdrift just ahead, there broke out two grouse that had been slumbering below. Away they went with a whirr, whirr, fast as wings could bear ·them.

But one was just a whit too slow; the springing Fox seized him in the air. At X he landed with him on the snow, and had a meal that, even in time of plenty, is a Fox's ideal; and now, in deep, hard winter, must have been a banquet of sheer delight.

Then, for the first time, I saw the meaning of the dead

A CHAPTER OF FOX LIFE

garter snake far back on the trail. Snake at no time is choice eating, and cold snake on a cold day must be a mighty cold meal. Clearly, the Fox thought so. He would rather take the chance of getting something better. He killed the snake so it could not get away. It was not likely that anyone would steal from him that unfragrant carcass, so he would come back and get it later if he must. But, as we see, he did not have to do so. His faith and patience were amply justified; for, instead of a cold, unpleasant snake, he fed that day on a fine hot bird.

Thus, I got a long, autobiographical chapter of Fox life by simply following his tracks through the snow. I never once saw the Fox himself that made it; and yet I know, and *you* know, it to be true as I have told it.

14 Tracks in Town

Most beginners are surprised to learn the abundance of opportunities for trailing in town.

Nearly all concrete pavements have in them the prints of Dogs and Cats that indiscreetly walked on the cement when it was fresh and soft. There are also a few tracks left by careless humans.

One of our ancient authorities tells us that the "proper study of mankind is man." With this thought guiding my activity, I have made many studies of human tracks, whose interest and usefulness increase as we learn their message.

As evidence, I give on page 103 some varied stories of human life that are recorded in footprints.

One might go still further in this field by taking up the kind of black-tracking that is known as *fingerprinting*. This is one of the most important kinds of tracking that has come into public notice and police practice; but it is a little outside our present plans and scope, since our chief interest is in following the ways of wild animals.

To illustrate the combination of wildlife and town life, I quote from my Journal the story of an invisible colony of furry creatures in a town, which story was told me solely by the tracks:

On February 5, 1902, as I walked up the main street of Malvern, Iowa, I was startled by seeing a familiar mark on the snow-covered street—the track of a Cottontail Rabbit. I searched around and found others. Of course, the main road showed nothing; but on the snow between sidewalk and roadway I found many of different sizes.

I took the surrounding neighborhood by blocks, and soon realized that the Rabbits were found only about the houses. Then the reason appeared: in the middle of each plot of land was a vegetable and truck garden. I expected to find some convenient runway between these gardens and the distant wooded country, but did not.

However, I soon saw that their chief places of refuge were the culverts and covered ditches, though several barns and lumber piles had Rabbit trails leading under them.

The people in the business blocks did not seem to know of the Rabbits' existence. But the Dogs undoubtedly did, for at one place I found evidence of a Dog-and-Rabbit race. At the end of it I found the tail and some of the skin of a Rabbit that had apparently made the mistake of venturing too far from the friendly culverts.

Thus, I satisfied myself of the existence of a colony of wild Cottontails living isolated in the midst of a town of five thousand inhabitants. The citizens seemed to know nothing of them, and I never saw one of them; yet my information was very nearly incontrovertible, and derived wholly from the tracks in the snow.

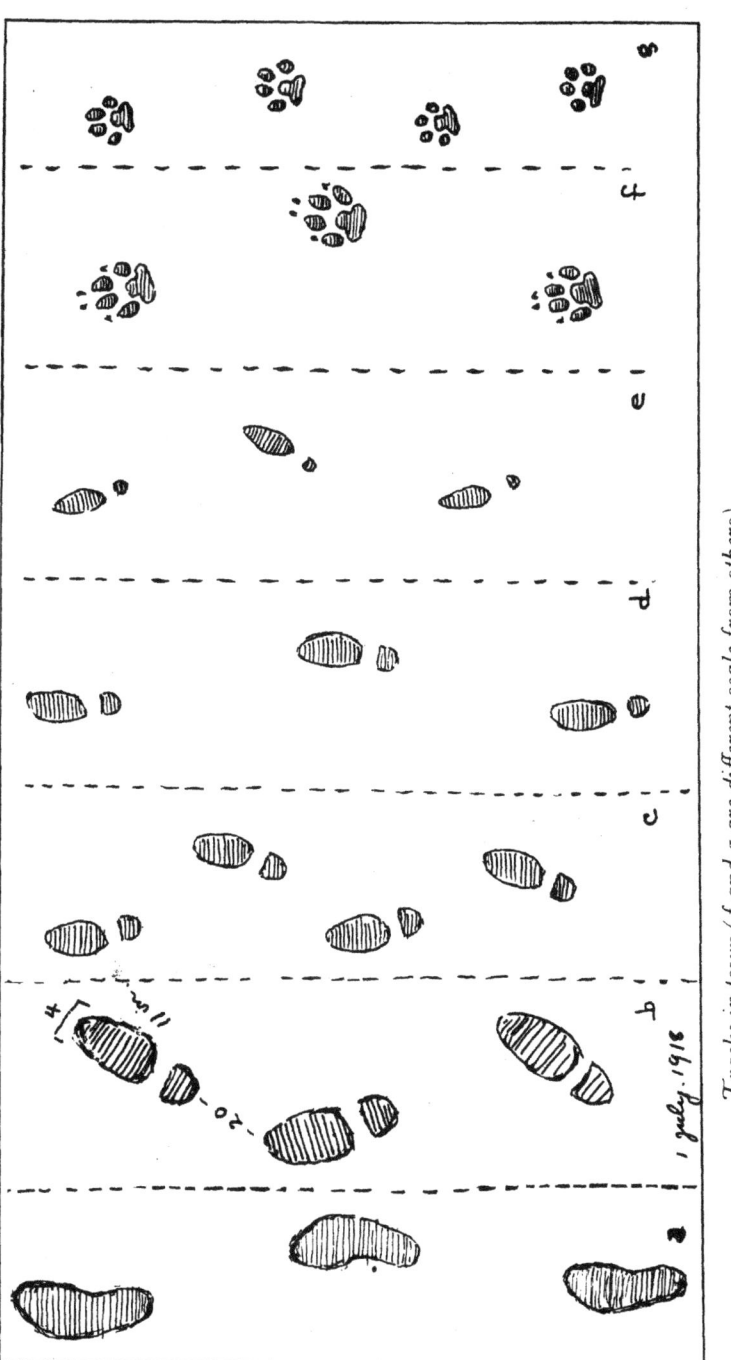

Tracks in loam (f and g are different scale from others)
a. A Sioux Indian   b. A white man   c. An old man (note the short steps).
d. A strong, active young fellow (note the straight set and long stride)
e. A young lady, slim and much turned out
f. A Dog (note the claws)   g. A Cat (no claws)

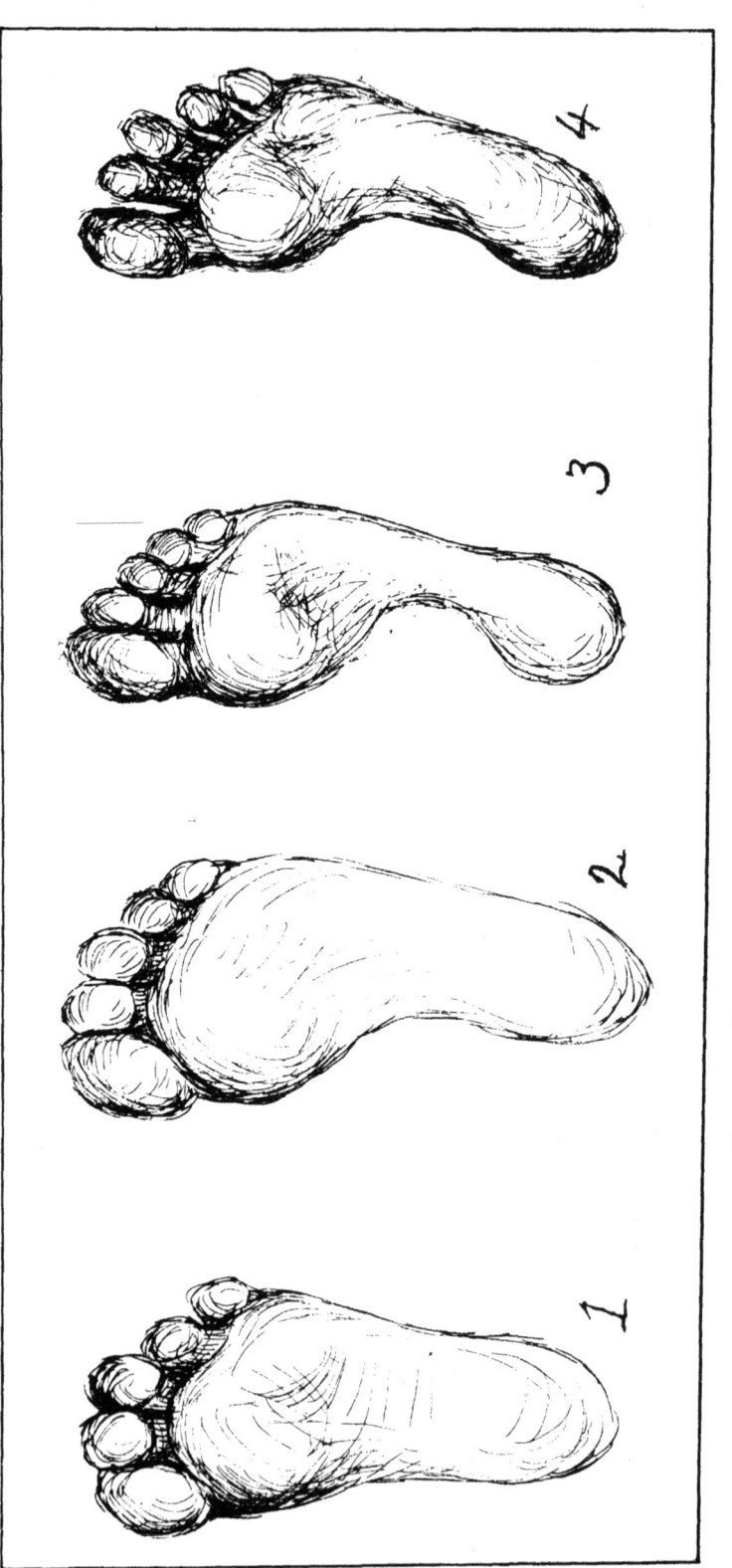

Human tracks
1. *A sturdy twelve-year-old boy who usually went barefoot*
2. *A sturdy twelve-year-old boy, barefoot sometimes; very muscular*
3. *A city man who always wore light boots, and never went barefoot*
4. *A tall, slender, athletic young man*

15 The Skunk and the Unwise Bobcat

As related in *Two Little Savages*, I early learned the trick of making autograph albums of mud or dust, so that the animals that came by in the night should leave me their names and maybe some sentiment suggested by their visit.

In the autumn of 1893, I was living in New Mexico, not far from Clayton. I made it my practice to sweep the dust smooth around my shanty each night, so that I could keep track of any four-footed visitors that might call. Of course, there were many blank nights; on others, the happenings were trifling. Some, however, were full of reward.

In this way I learned of the Coyote's visits to the garbage pail, of the Skunk establishment under the house, and other interesting facts as in the diagrams (Pages 106 and 108).

One night I had been aroused by a strong smell of Skunk, followed by strange muffled sounds that soon died away. So forth I went at sunrise, and found the odor of Skunk no dream, but a stern reality. Then reference to my

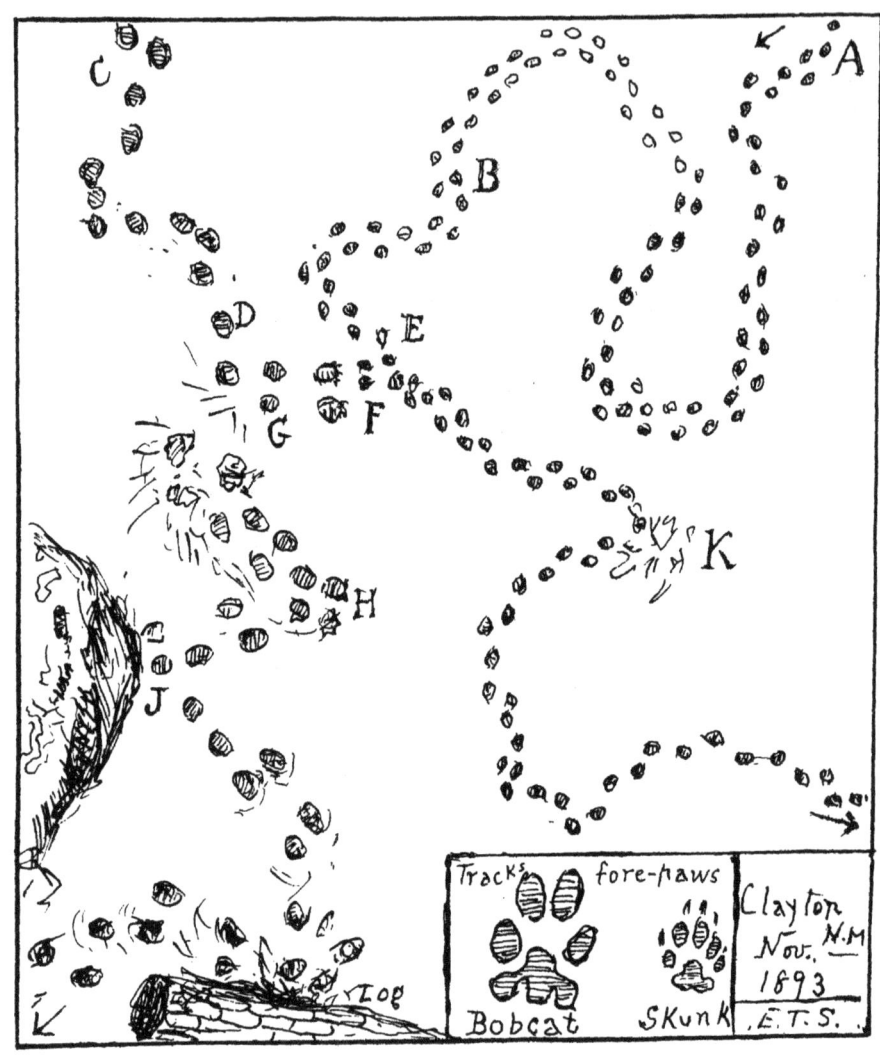

The unwise Bobcat

THE SKUNK AND THE UNWISE BOBCAT

dust album revealed an inscription which, after a little condensing and clearing up, appeared much as on page 106.

At A, a Skunk had come on the scene. At B, he was wandering about when a hungry Wildcat or Bobcat Lynx appeared (C). Noting the promise of something to kill for food, the latter came on at D. The Skunk, observing the intruder, said: "You better let me alone"; and not wishing to make trouble, moved off toward E.

But the Bobcat, evidently young and inexperienced, gave chase. At F the Skunk wheeled about, remarking: "Well, if you will have it, here goes!"

At G the Lynx was hit; the mad rush from G to H shows the effect. At J the Cat bumped into a stone, indicating probably that he was blinded; then ricocheted into a log (L), after which he went bouncing and bounding away.

The Skunk merely said: "I told you so!" then calmly resumed the even tenor of his way. At K he found the remains of a chicken, on which he feasted, and went quietly home to bed.

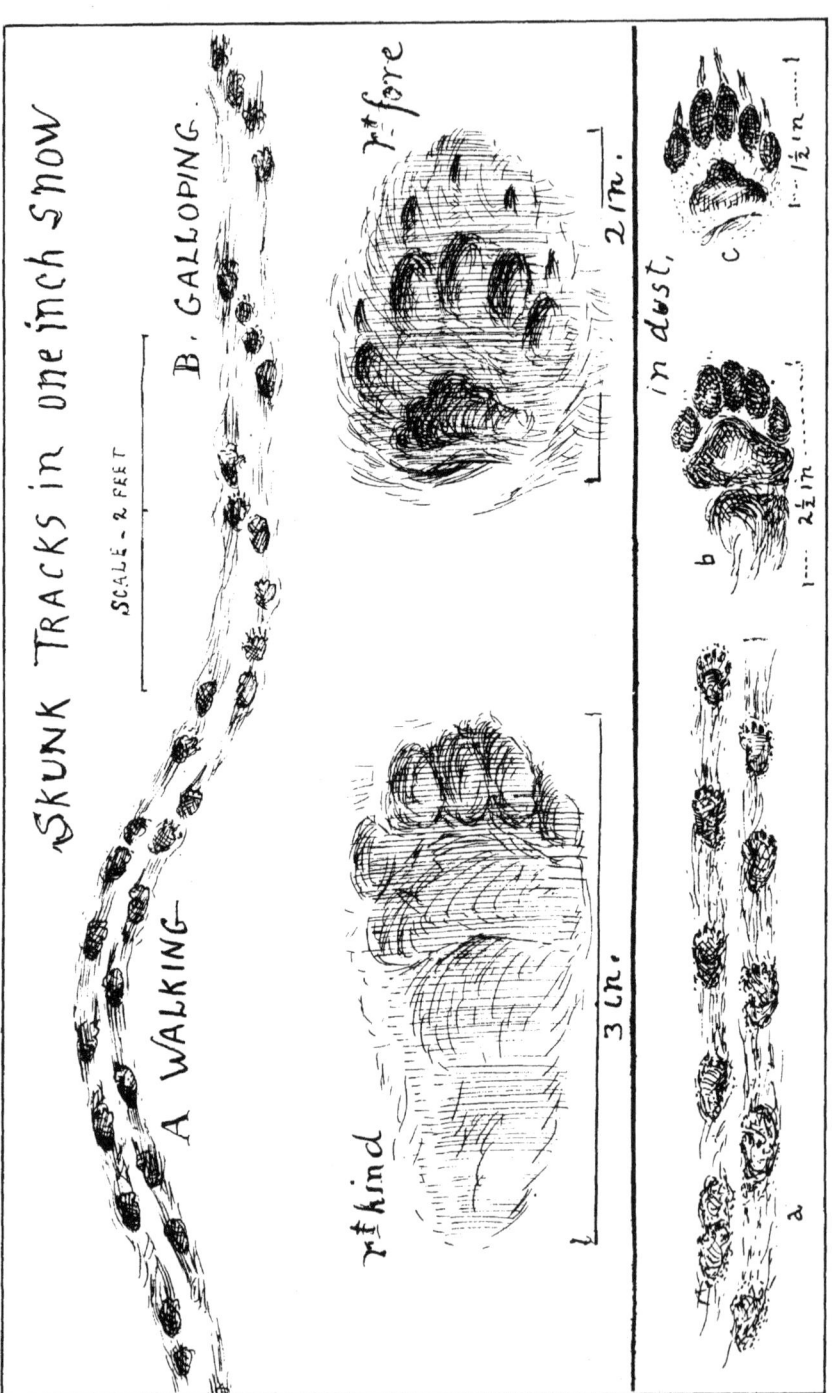

Tracks of Common Skunk

16 The Dude on the Trail

Long ago, in the backwoods of Canada, I met an enthusiastic English dude who gave me some good laughs. He went out after the first fall of snow, determined to be a real hunter and to discover for himself the secrets of the trail.

Of course, he soon found a Rabbit track and shrewdly guessed that it was a Deer track, the two long marks being, he assumed, the prints of the main hoofs, the lesser ones the clouts or accessory hoofs, which are higher up behind and much smaller.

It was only after that Rabbit had led him through many small holes in the fence, and at last into an underground burrow, that he would believe the old farmer who told him it was a Rabbit track.

Equipped with this new knowledge, he now ran swiftly along a fresh Rabbit trail, believing that he could run the creature down. But here he made another bad guess.

He knew that the bigger tracks were made by the Rabbit's hind feet; therefore, since the smaller tracks were always to the east of the larger ones, this Rabbit must be running toward the east. Alas! He had yet to learn that a speeding Rabbit overreaches at each bound, so that the hind feet track ahead of the fore feet. This Rabbit was really running west; but the young hunter followed backward for an hour or more, and of course saw nary a Rabbit.

17 Dabbles the Coon

One day, as I walked by a Canadian stream, I saw a track like those on page 112. In eastern North America, this is not likely to be mistaken for that of any species other than a Raccoon.

Realizing, then, that this was his hunting ground, I set about looking for his home. I knew it was likely to be in some nearby hollow tree. Knowing further that trees which are hollow have either a big scar on one side or a dead top, I examined each tree that showed these signs.

At last I found some Coon hairs—only two or three—on the bark of one tree, and felt sure that I had located my Coon's earth. But, to make sure, I wiped out the track along the creek and smoothed the dust, so as to be ready for his next tracks.

In the morning—for the Coon is a night prowler—I found that not only an old Coon but several little ones had come down the tree and had gone a-frog-hunting up the stream, leaving in their tracks a plain record. It is not easy

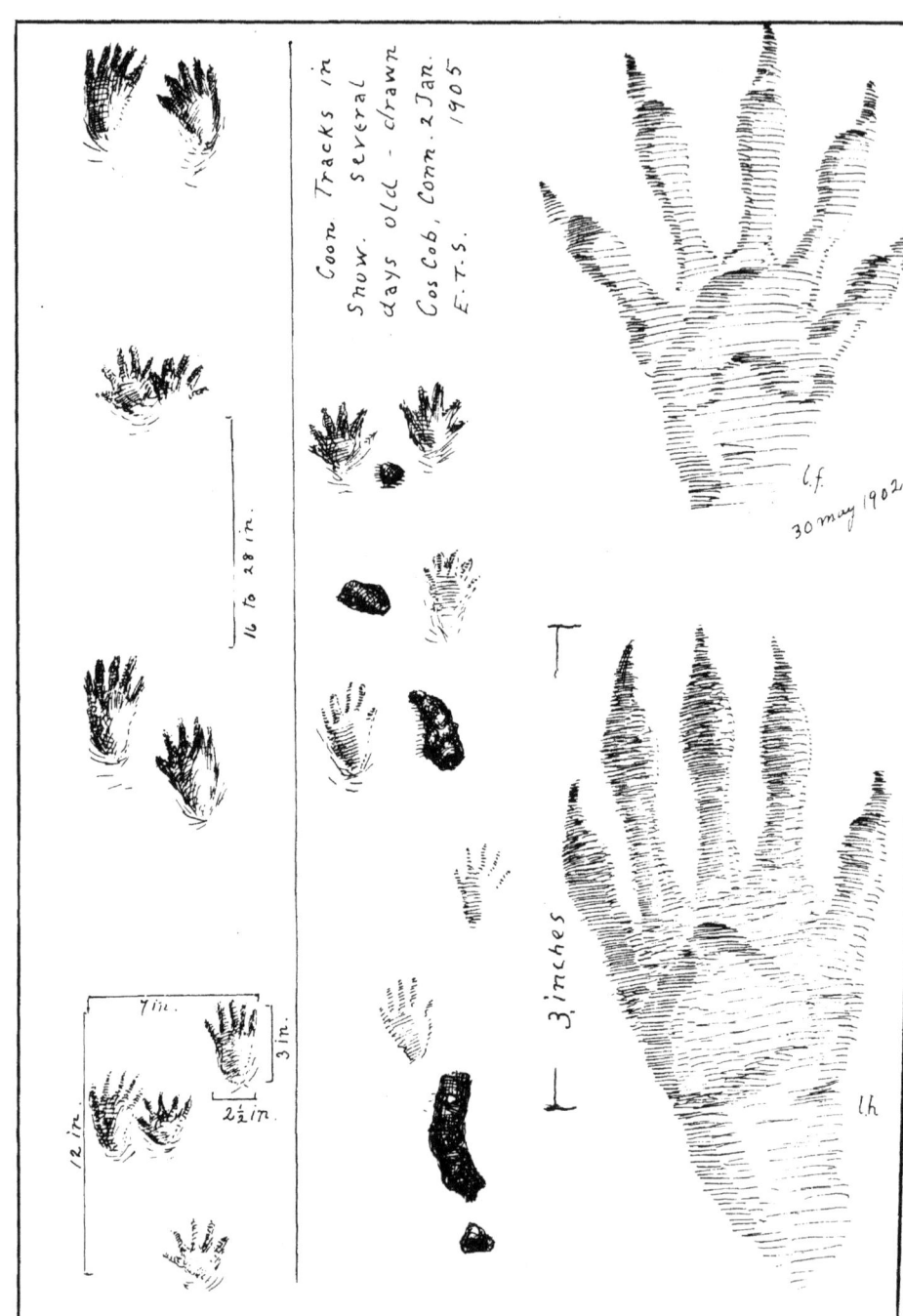

Life of a Coon

to say how many creatures of a kind are about when the tracks are numerous, but I felt sure that I had found the home of a mother Coon and her two or three young ones.

I saw their tracks many times after this, and began to feel that I was getting acquainted with them, although I had never seen any of the animals themselves. The nearest to actual meeting was hearing the long-drawn whicker of the old Coon once or twice at night.

In the neighborhood was a half-breed squatter known as "Injun Pete." Sometimes I used to talk with him about animals in general. Although a good-for-nothing character, he had considerable knowledge of wildlife.

I did not tell him anything about my Coon friends; but one day he remarked to me: "There's a family of Coons up in the woods; I see their tracks along the creek. I reckon I'll get them all when they are big enough."

"Now see here," I said. "I found those Coons first; I know where they live, and I want you to let them alone."

"I guess they're mine as much as yourn till they are ketched," said Pete, "but I won't bother them for a while anyway."

So I continued to smooth out the mud and dust for my Coons each night to write accounts of their visits; and thus I got much of the information which I afterward put together into the story that appeared under the title "Dabbles the Coon."

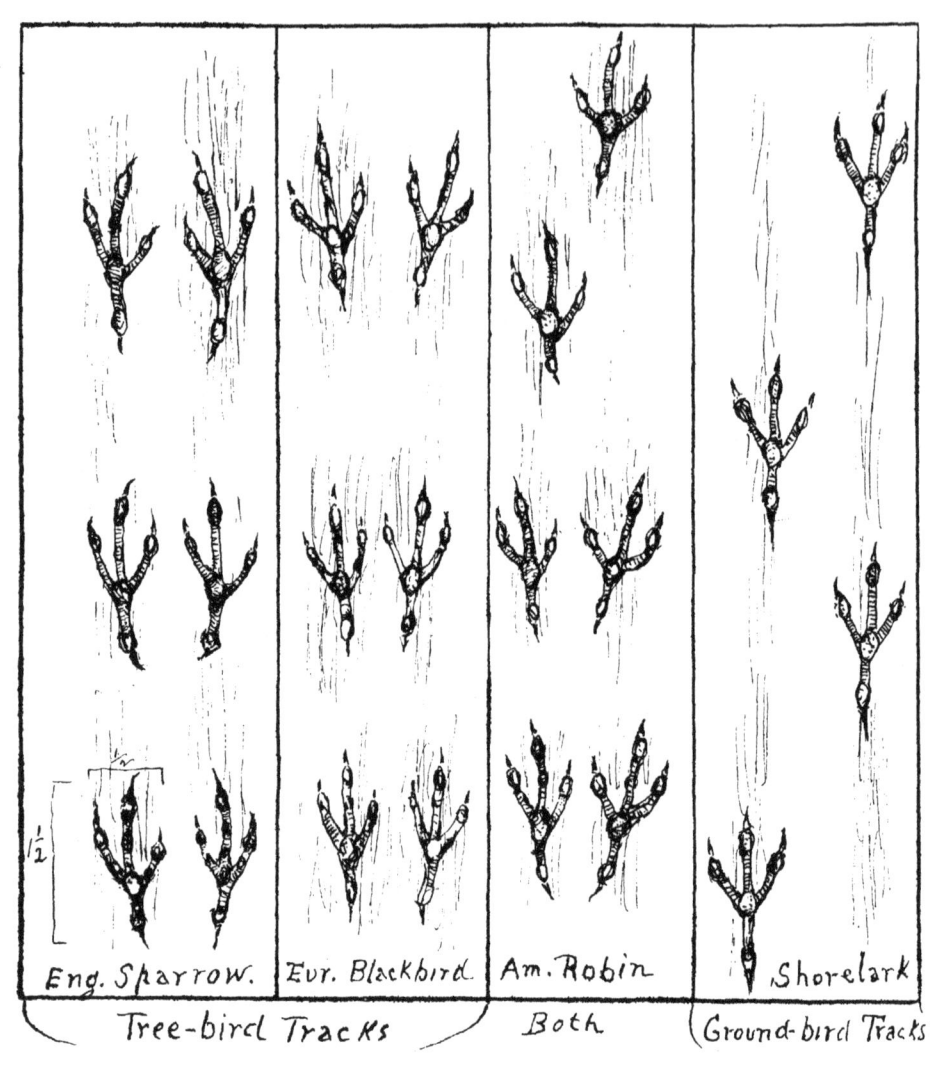

Various birds

18 Deer and Antelope Tracks

Of the Deer, the common Whitetail or Virginia Deer is the species which is best known. It is, indeed, the most widely dispersed of all the small Deer, covering the entire United States except the desert States and the Pacific coast. Its tracks are not distinguishable with certainty from those of the other small Deer.

Throughout the Northwest I found a popular tradition that a dwarf Deer inhabited the brushy arroyos of the upper Missouri Valley. In most cases, this dwarf or Gazelle Deer turned out to be the fawn of either the Whitetail or the Mule Deer.

There is, however, a very small Deer in Mexico and in our own States near the border, which is known as the Mexican Deer. The tracks of this one are much like the fawn tracks at the bottom of page 117. This Deer is scientifically known as *Odocoileus virginianus couesi;* and even when adult, is said to weigh less than sixty pounds.

In the early '80s, the Antelope abounded on the dry plains and upland prairies of the West. There is no way now of gauging their numbers, but they probably exceeded the number of domestic Sheep that are now occupying their ancient homeland.

In my cow-punching days—that is, 1893 and 1894—I rode the range daily on the Canadian River of Texas. We saw everywhere flocks of domestic Sheep which had already invaded the Cattle country in great numbers. Yet I think we saw more herds of Antelope; and so far as guess has value, they on the whole outnumbered the Sheep.

The Sheep population of the United States in 1900 is given at approximately thirty million; so that it is probable that the Antelope, in their pristine numbers, equaled this official enumeration of the Sheep. Another computation, with more complete data, sets their number as high as forty million.

Alas! What a change today! The Antelope that now exist do so by grace of vigilant game wardens. Nevertheless, they are yet to be found; and one may still get a permit to go forth in the right season to secure a buck Antelope.

Among the anatomical peculiarities that have given the species a unique place in zoology is the absence of clouts or hind hoofs. That is to say, while all of the Deer family have on each foot four digits with a hoof on each, the Antelope has but two—a fact which sometimes is recorded in the tracks, especially when these were made by the creature walking through mud that is four or five inches deep (Page 118).

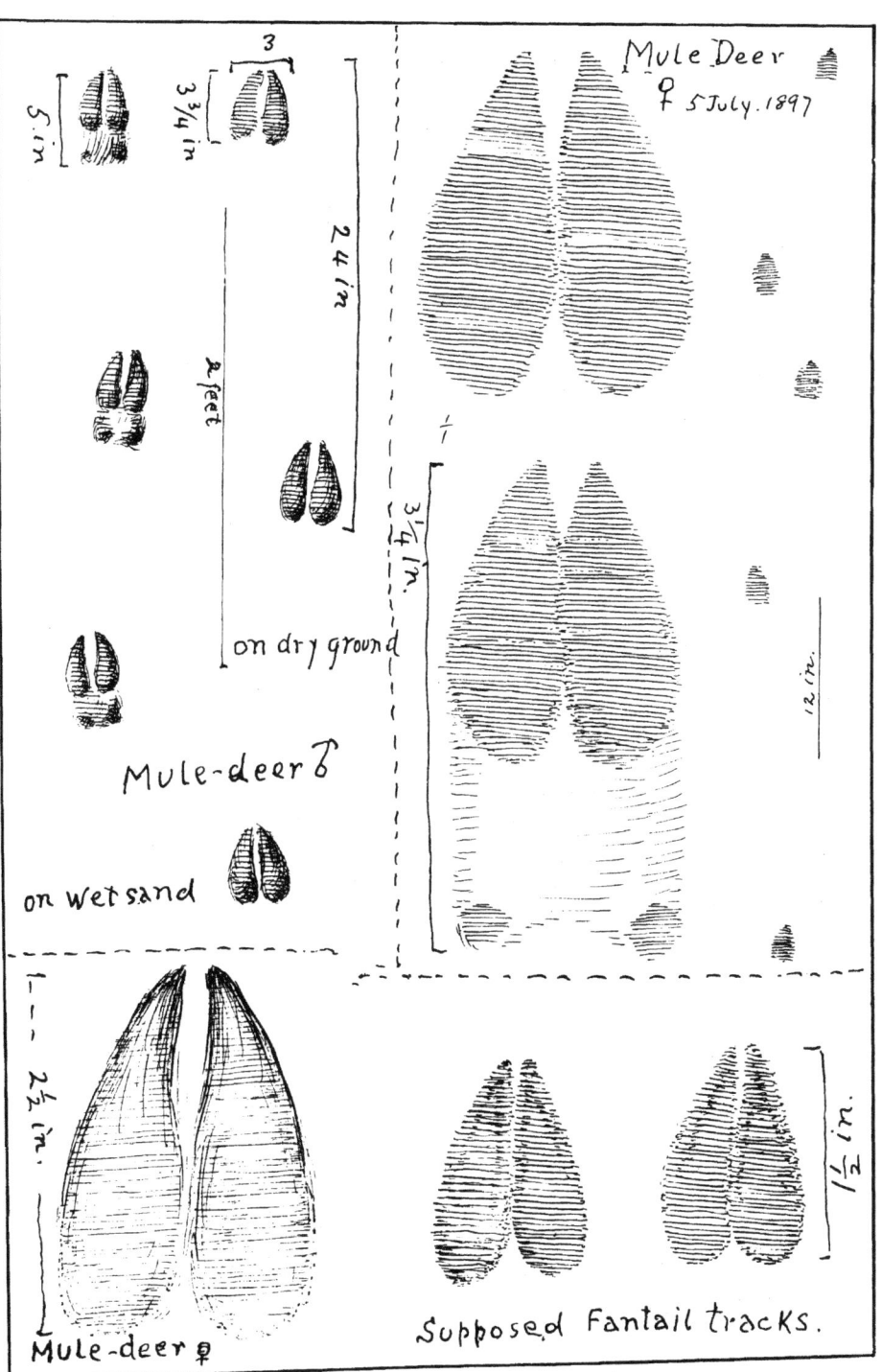

Tracks of Mule Deer

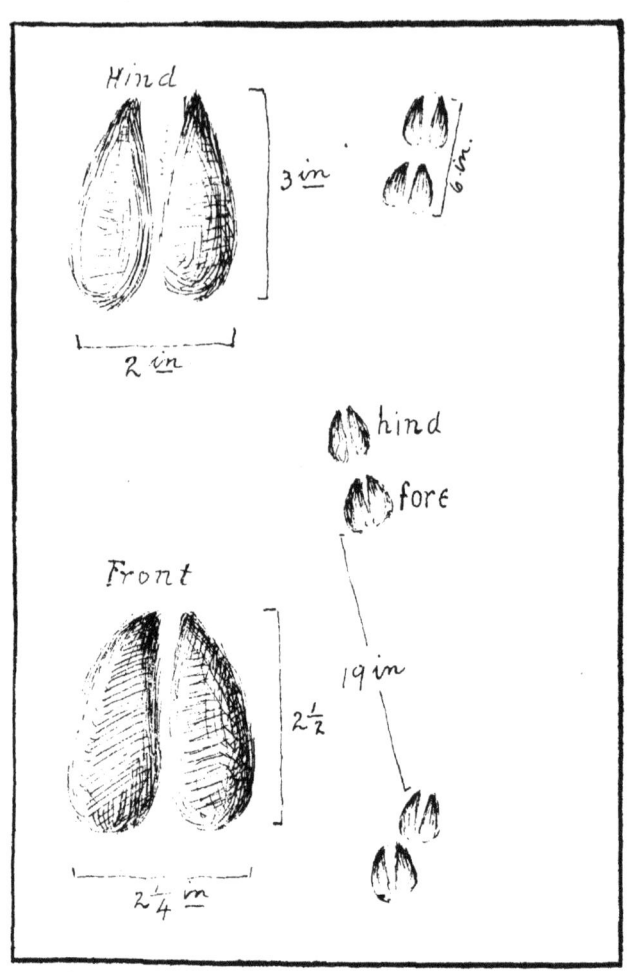

Tracks of large Antelope

19 Some Northern Animals

If we divide the continent arbitrarily into northern and southern regions, we shall find that the vast majority of the large and worth-while game animals belong to the northern or colder parts. Sportsmen may go South for small game, especially for waterfowl; but nearly all the big game is found in the northern States and in Canada.

Following this unscientific grouping, I give, for the benefit of the hunter, a number of the important big game tracks that opportunely came my way, viz:

Moose (pages 120 and 121); Musk Ox (page 122); Wood Buffalo (page 123); Woodland Caribou (page 124); Barrenground Caribou (page 124); Elk (page 125); Grizzly Bear (page 128); Kodiak Bear (page 128); Black Bear (page 128); to which I add, simply because they are boreal, the small but important Marten (pages 126 and 127), and the Snowshoe Rabbit (page 129).

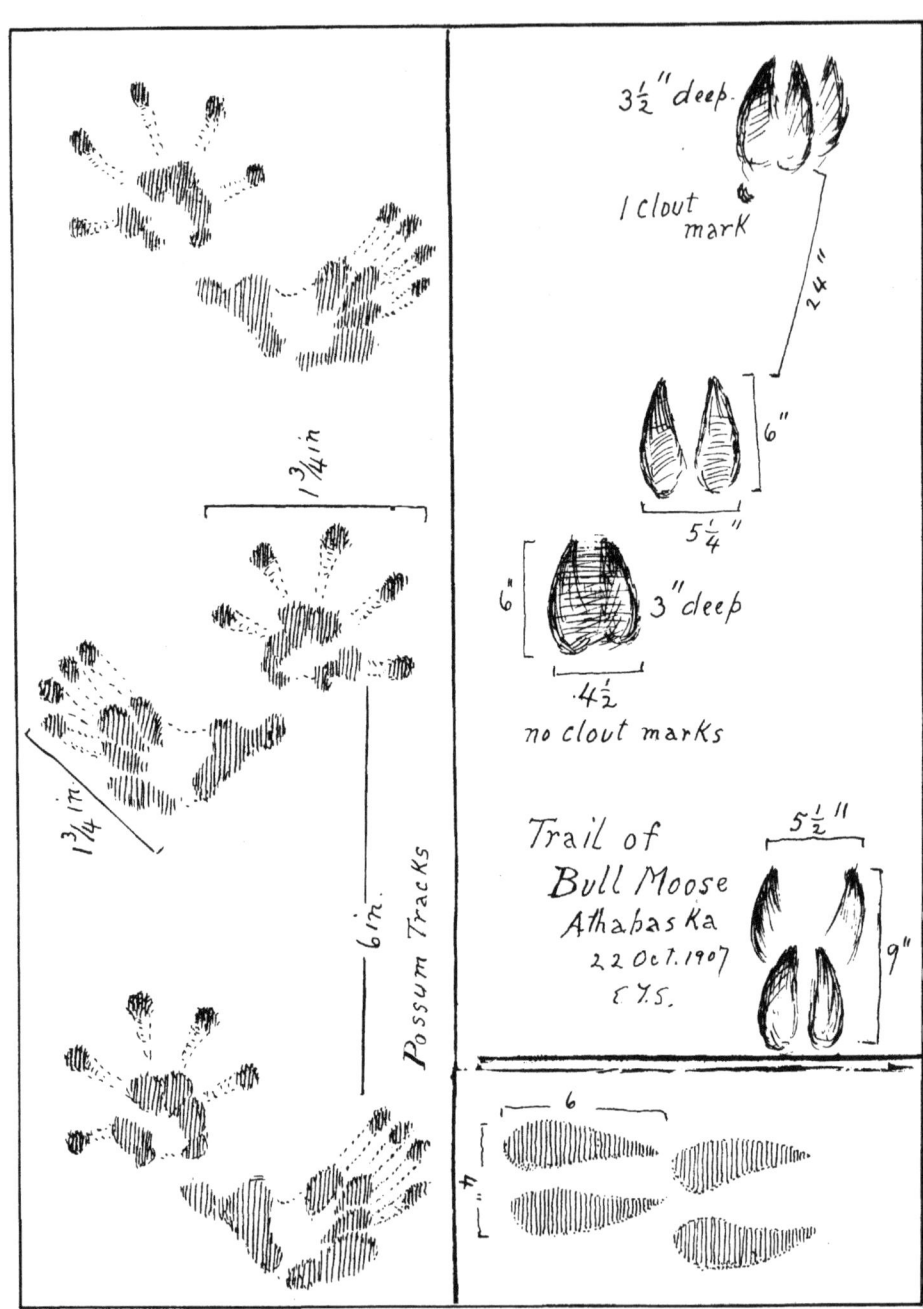

Bull Moose and Possum tracks

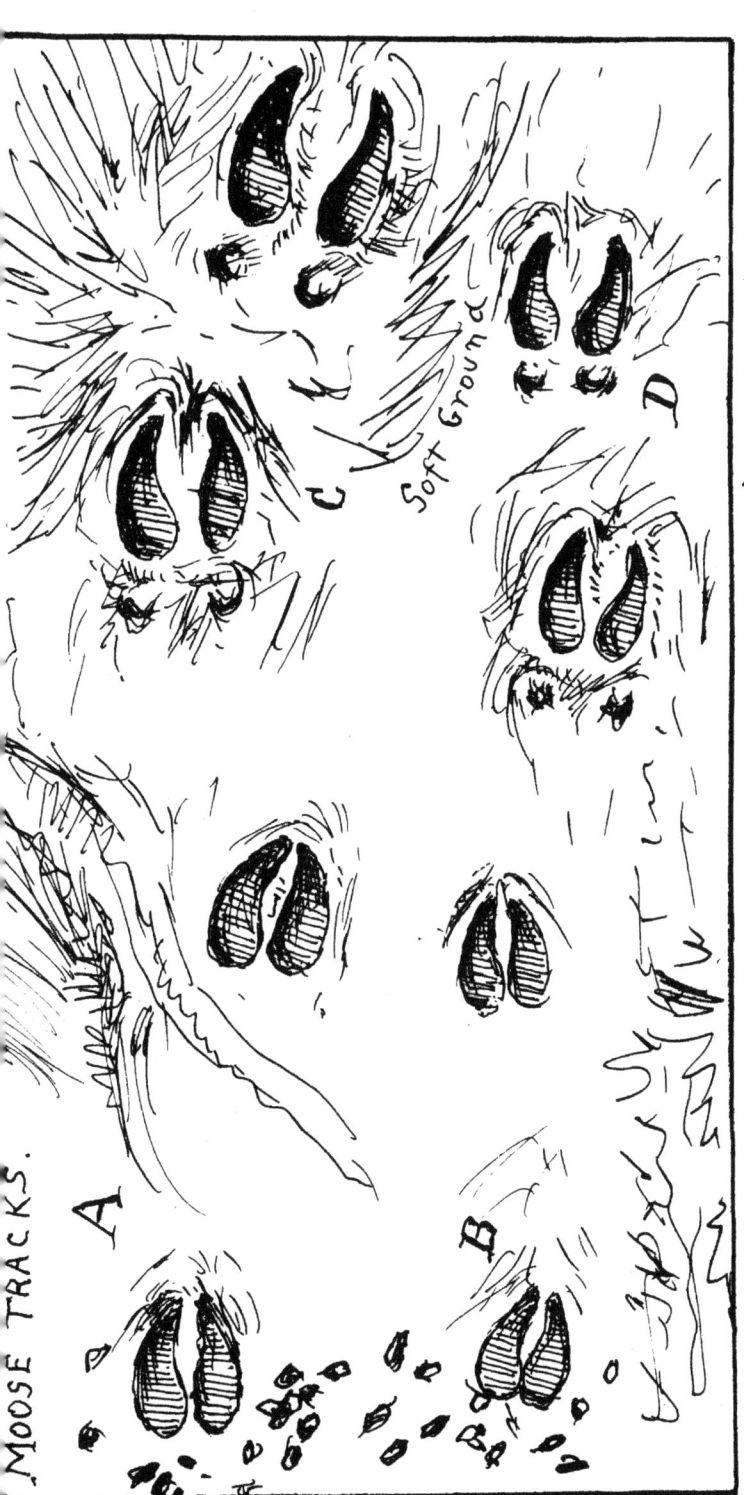

Moose tracks. Bull (A) and Cow (B) in about one inch of snow. The Bull tracks are 5 x 6 inches; the strides vary from 2 feet to 5 feet. At C and D the softer ground and deeper snow cause the toes to spread and the hind hoofs or clouts to show. The Cow track (B) is distinguished by the smaller size (4 x 5½ inches) and slenderer form

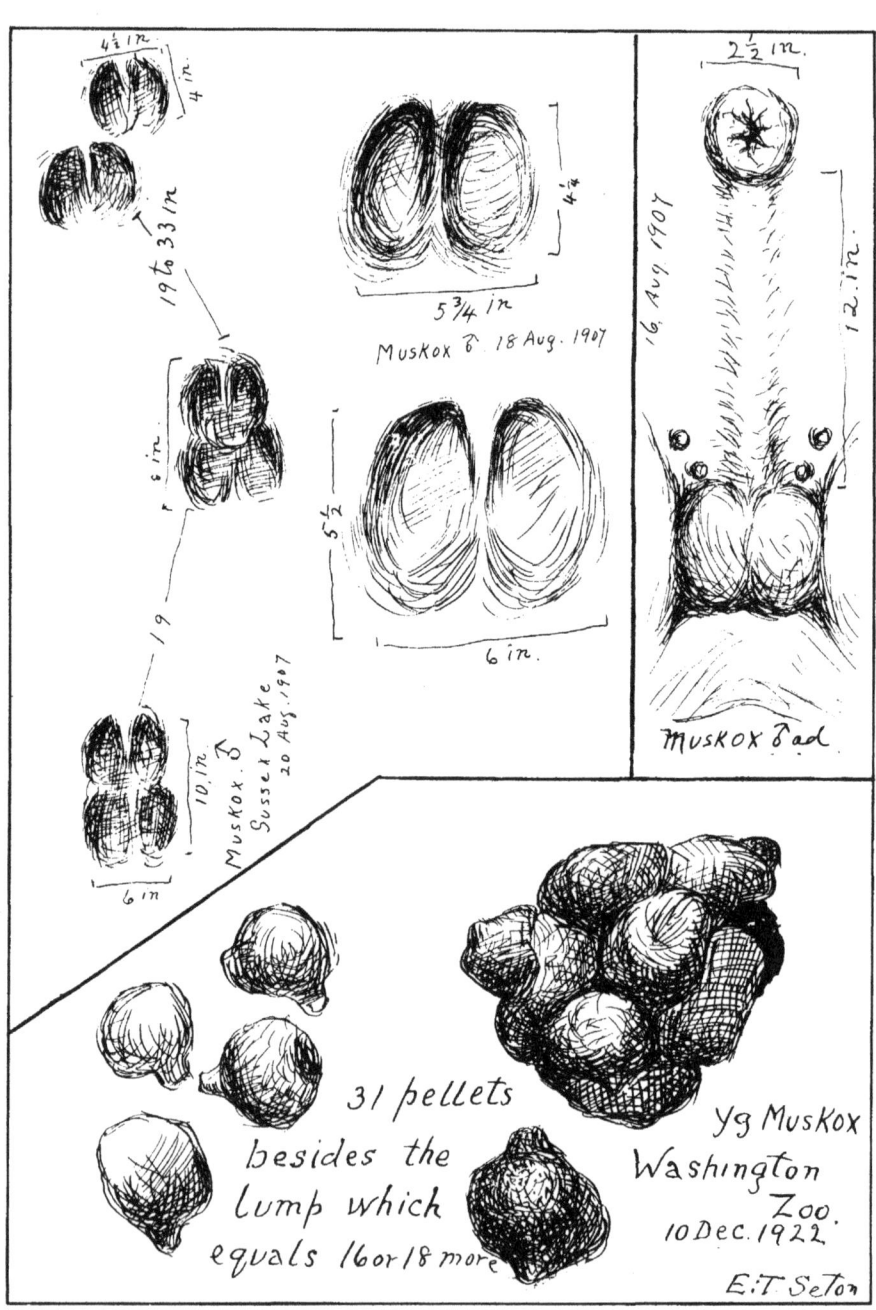

Musk Ox details

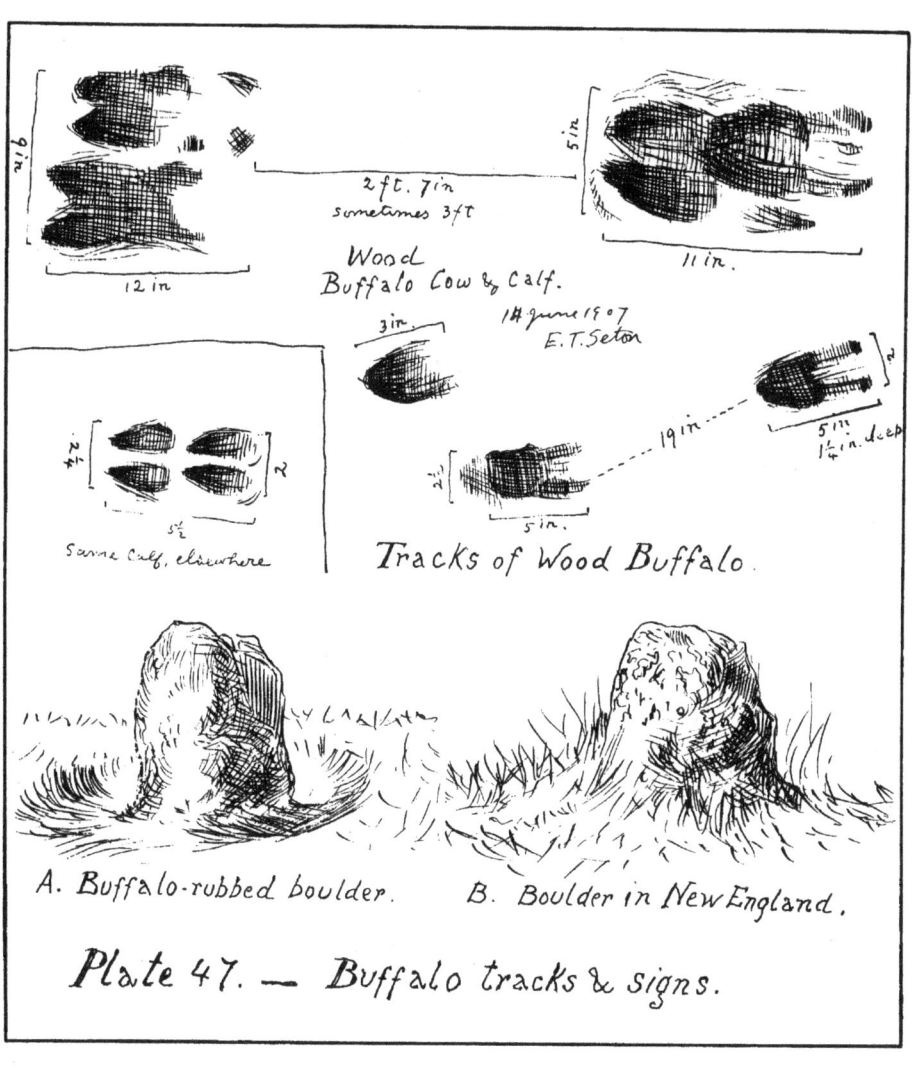

Buffalo tracks and signs

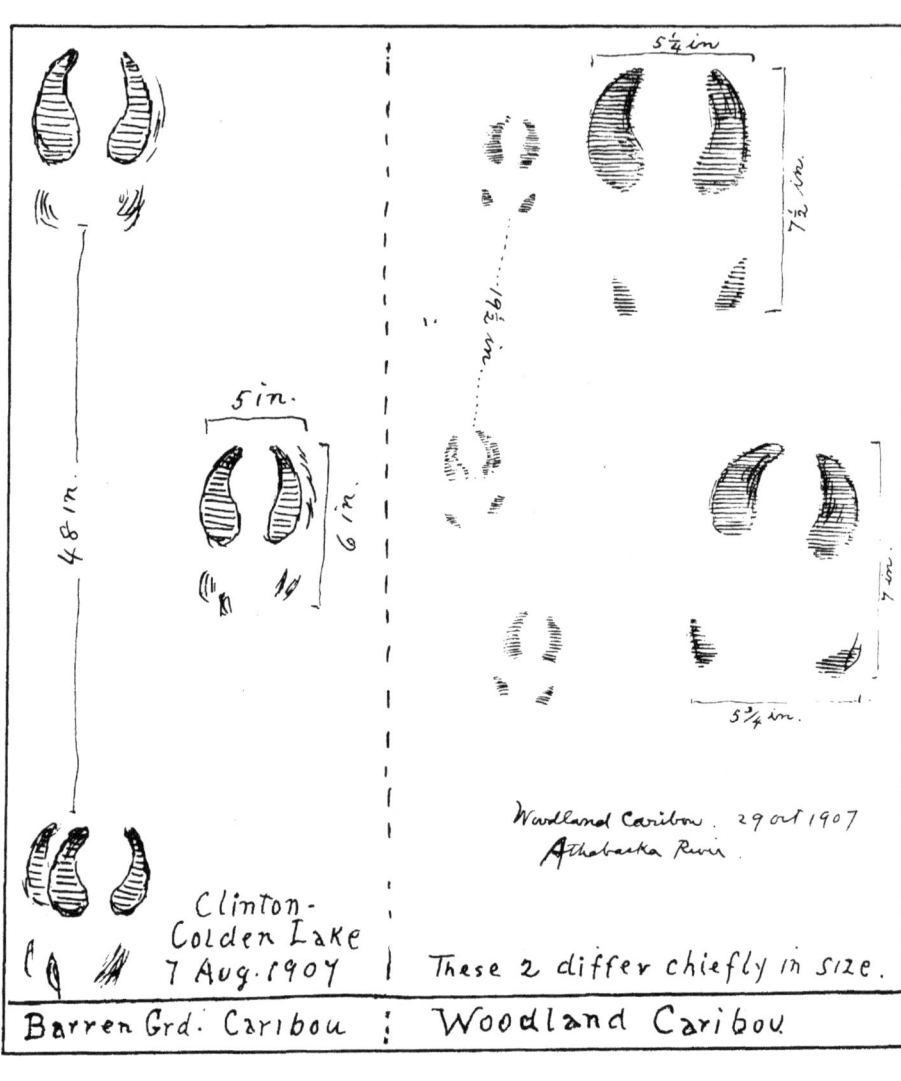

Tracks of Caribou

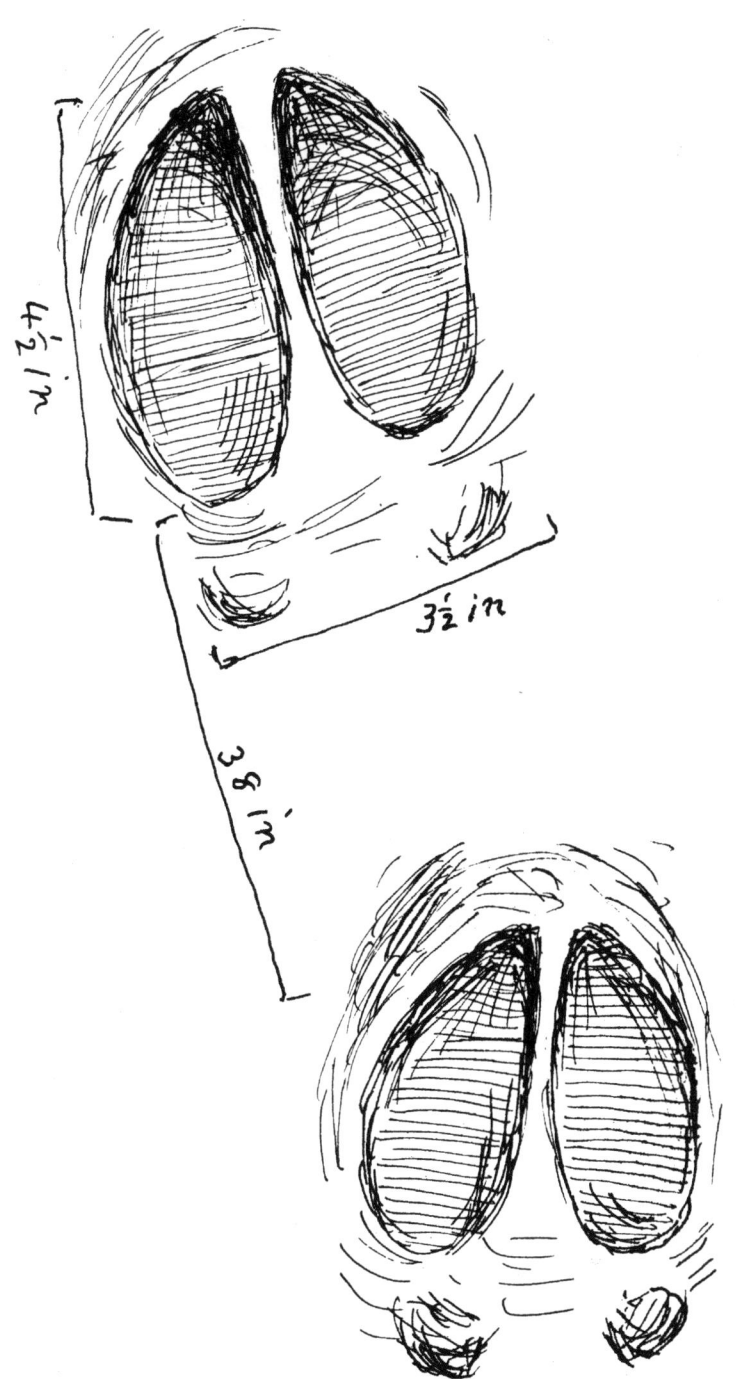

Bull ELK.
in 4 in. snow
17 Sep. 1902

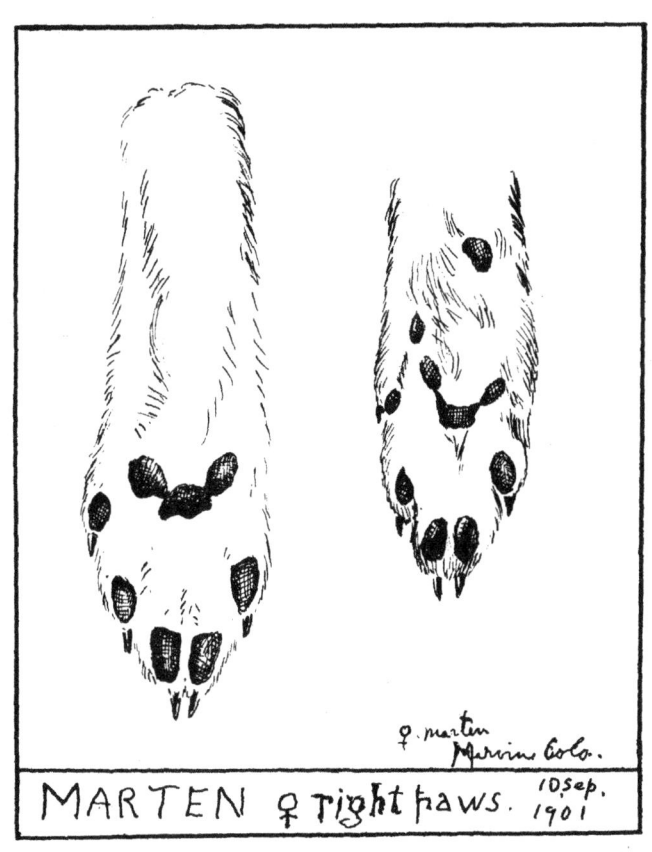

Paws of Marten

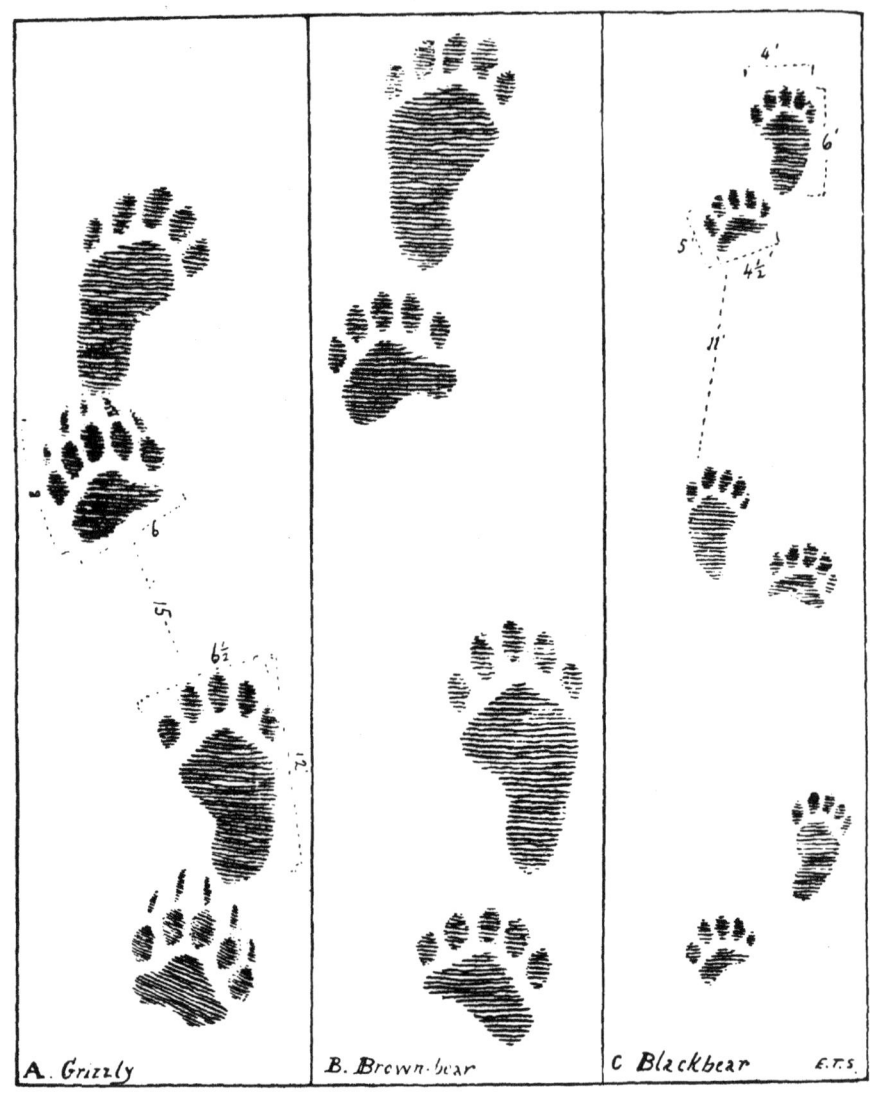

Tracks: A. Grizzly. Yellowstone Park, Sept. 7, 1912
B. Kodiak Brown Bear. Washington Zoo
C. Black Bear. Athabaska River. Sept. 30, 1901
The chief differences are in size; also the Grizzly often shows claws.

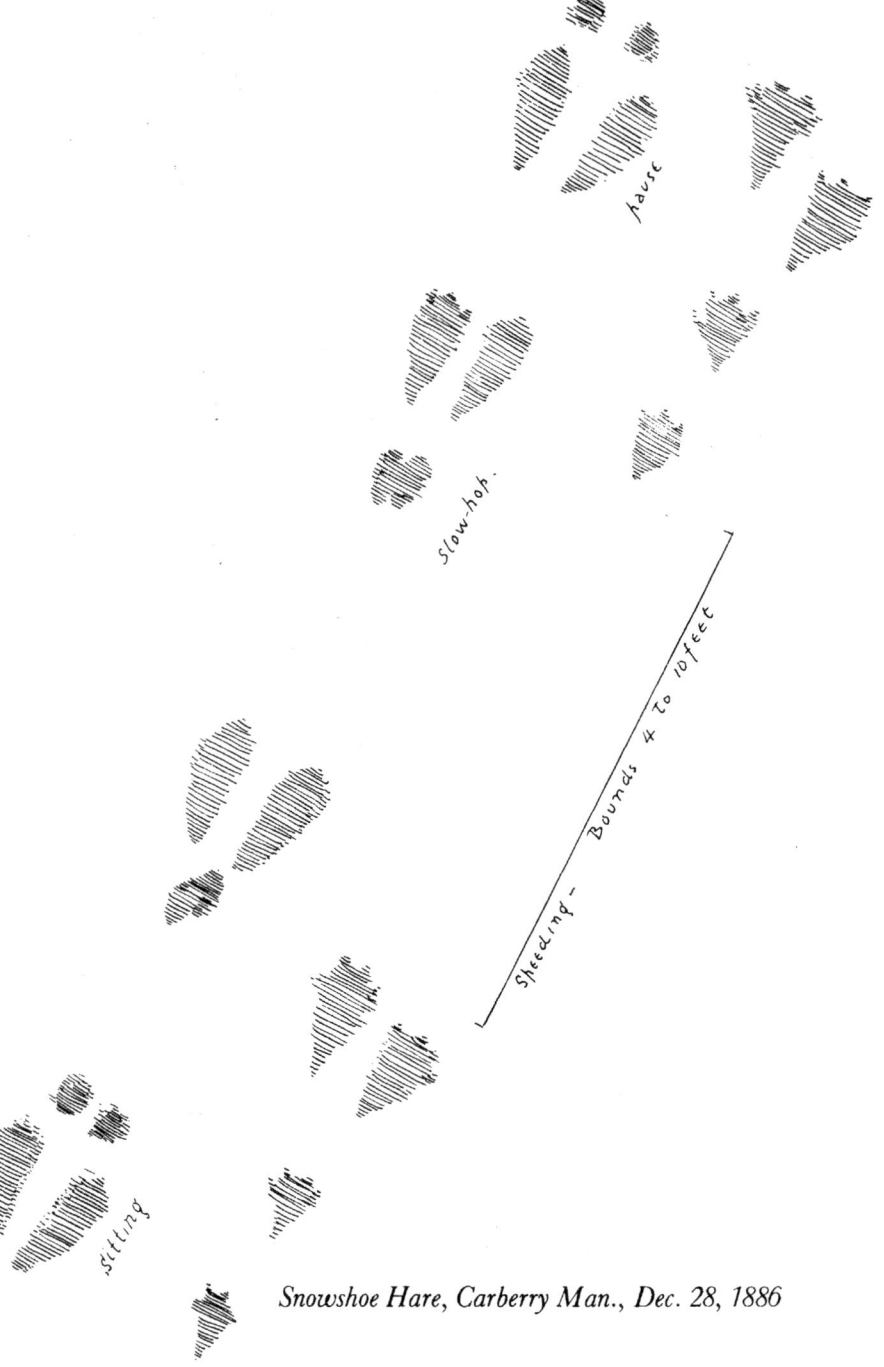

Snowshoe Hare, Carberry Man., Dec. 28, 1886

20 Scats or Signs

Scatology, i.e., the study of scats or dung pellets, has never had formal consideration as a definite department of zoology. Every field naturalist or hunter appreciates the fact that, after the animal itself, the scats and the tracks together afford the most definite information on the habits, food, and whereabouts of the creature.

I know of no attempt, outside of my *Life Histories* (1909), and my *Lives of Game Animals* (1925-28), to picture and discuss these interesting and material records—oftentimes the only records we have of the presence of certain animals.

Among hunters, they are usually called "sign"; and in some communities and polite literature they are called "visiting cards" or "cards," for obvious reasons.

When they are approached as a basis of classification, I find that the form and substance of the scats is an excellent—yes, a quite reliable—guide to the *order* of a creature. Thus, all of the *Pachyderms* have their rectal output of the same type and nearly the same color, substance, and odor as that of the Horse; while a similar kinship is shown among those of the *ruminants*. Those of *Carnivora, Rodentia, Insectivora,* etc., show a style that clearly and exclusively belongs to the *order* in question, and is a reflex of its peculiar anatomy.

Accepting the form of the dung pellets as a diagnostic of ordinal value, the simplicident rodents (or Rats) and the duplicident rodents (or Rabbits) are of wholly different *orders*. The Sheep and the Deer, however, would, by this test, be lumped as one.

As a *family* feature, the scatology has little value; and as a *generic* feature, none whatever. But now we meet with a surprise. Though useless as a generic index, the scats are extremely valuable and helpful as a specific character, because here we receive to the full the helpful information of size and constituents.

Thus, the output of Fox and Wolf may be of precisely the same form; but their identity will be settled by the great difference in size and the fact that the product of the Fox will contain more or less Mouse traces, whereas that of the

ON OPPOSITE PAGE

Scatology of the Deer. All pellets are on the same scale, 100 to 200 at each place

1.–7. Wapiti; 1. and 2., spring; 3. summer, all green grass; 4. and 5. autumn, dry grass and twigs; 6. winter, nearly all woody fiber; 7. gravel and sand, doubtless swallowed medicinally

8.–11. Mule-Blacktail. 8. Buck; 9. and 10. adult, probably doe; 11 fawn. 12. Whitetail, not distinguishable from those of Blacktail and sometimes as large as those of Wapiti. Mar. 16, 1899

14. Caribou, Athabaska River, Oct. 30, 1907

15. Moose. Though sometimes confluent in green-grass season, these are typical and easily known. Aug. 29, 1904

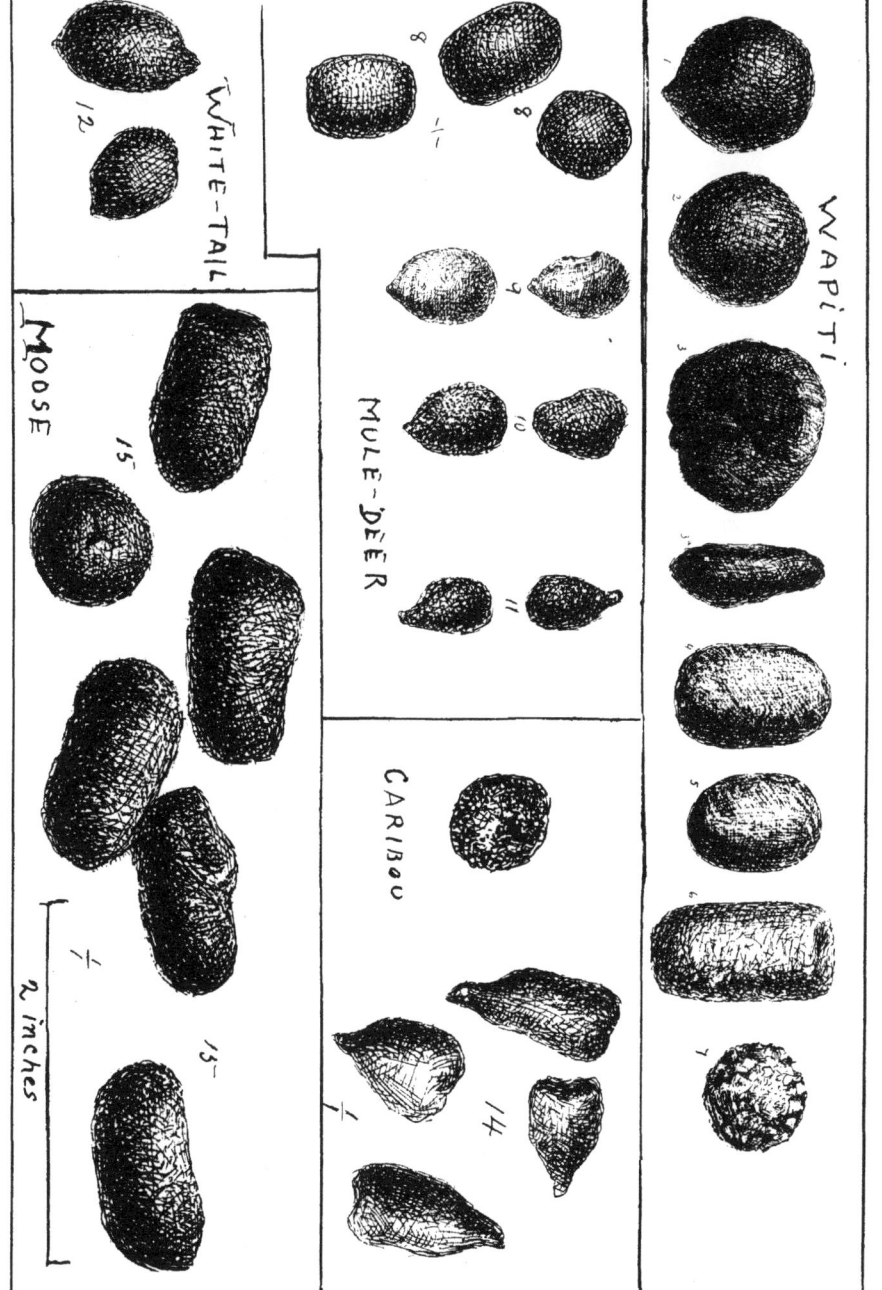

Scatology of certain Rodents
  a. *Richardson Ground Squirrel*
  b. *Thirteen-striped Ground Squirrel*
  c. *Carolina Gray Squirrel*
  d. *Southern Flying Squirrel* (volans)
  e. *House Rat, living in the woods*
  f. *House Mouse*
  g. *Connecticut, Deer Mouse* (noveboracensis)
     x. *Fed on bread, etc.*
     xx. *Different individual the night after capture*
     xxx. *Same as last, nut-fed for days*
  h. *Drummond Vole*
  i. *A great pile found in the woods at Cos Cob, evidently dating from winter, probably* Microtus pinetorum
  j. Synaptomys cooperi? *Ottawa River*
  k. *Pocket Gopher* (T. fossor)
  l. *Beaver, all woody fiber*
  m. *Snowshoe Rabbit (winter)*
  n. *Porcupine, 3 different individuals, the large (b) wild, the others (a, c) captive*
  o. *Woodchuck in October*
  p. *Common Prairie Dog*
  q. *Muskrat, September*

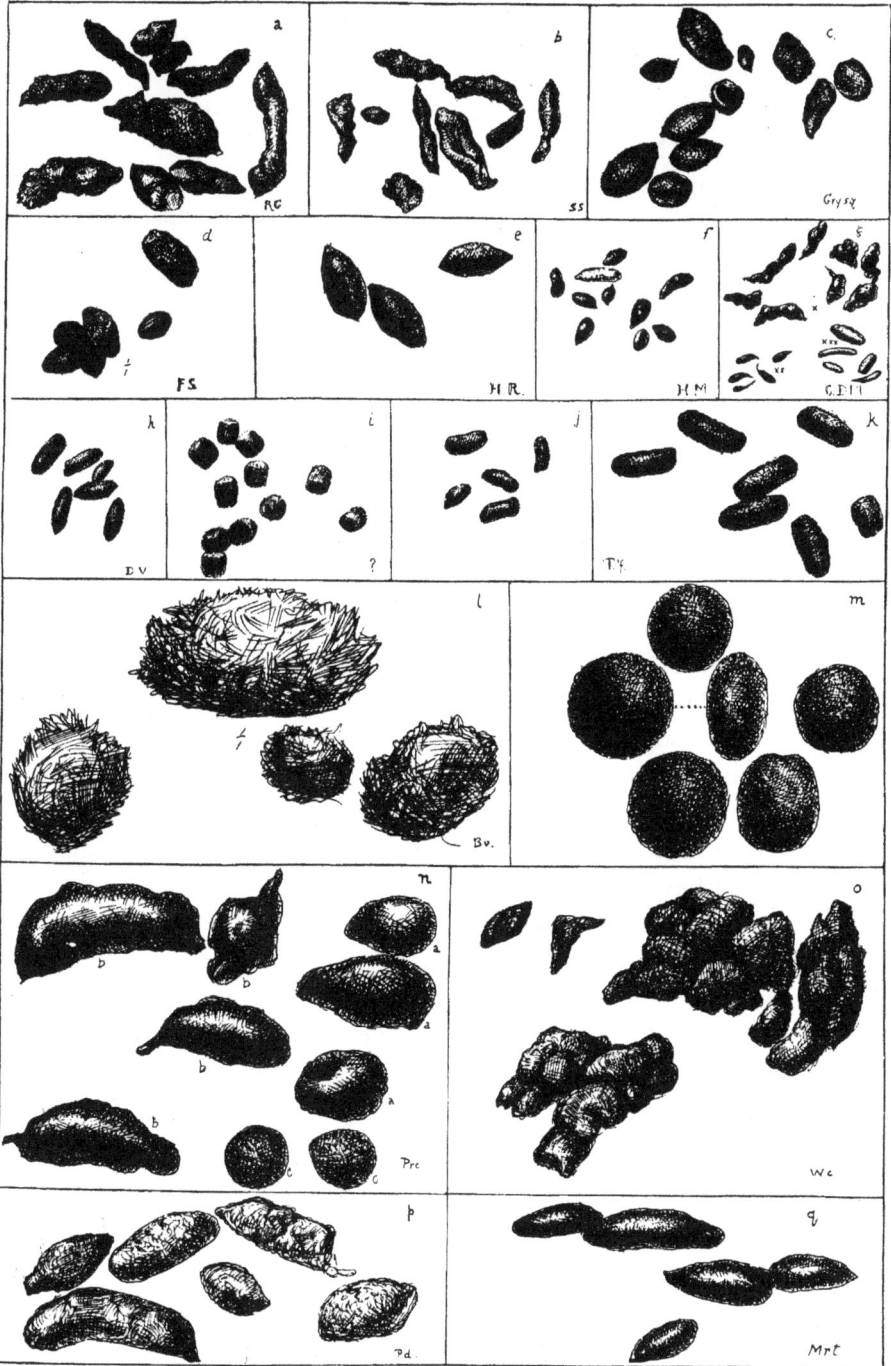

Wolf will show the remains of Deer and Cattle to the exclusion of Mice.

Again, Lynx and Fox scats may be of exactly the same size and color; but the presence of seeds, berries, or insects in the latter, and the exclusively animal nature of the former, help to a satisfactory decision.

The disposal of the scats—that is, the creature's slow, blind gropings toward sanitation—opens up another most interesting subject. There are two, or perhaps three, established systems to effect this, all three long known in the animal world, but very recent among ourselves. These are the "wet system," the "dry system," and the "parasitic system."

THE WET SYSTEM

A pair of Uinta Bobcats that I kept in my menagerie for over a year were very careful about their sanitation; at least, I suppose they thought so. Regularly, after their morning drink, they turned about and carefully dropped their excretes in the water trough. In this case, the procedure was, of course, unclean; but in natural surroundings would have been quite correct, for our engineers assure us that *sufficient dilution is disinfection.*

The principle is clearly recognized also in a Mosaic ordinance. After listing a vast number of things as "unclean," and stating that any of these falling into a drinking vessel pollute it with its contents, so both must be destroyed, the great Lawgiver adds: "Nevertheless, a fountain or pit wherein there is plenty of water, shall continue clean" (Leviticus 11: 36).

THE DRY SYSTEM

The dry-earth plan is that of the many creatures who bury their dung. The highest development of this is seen among

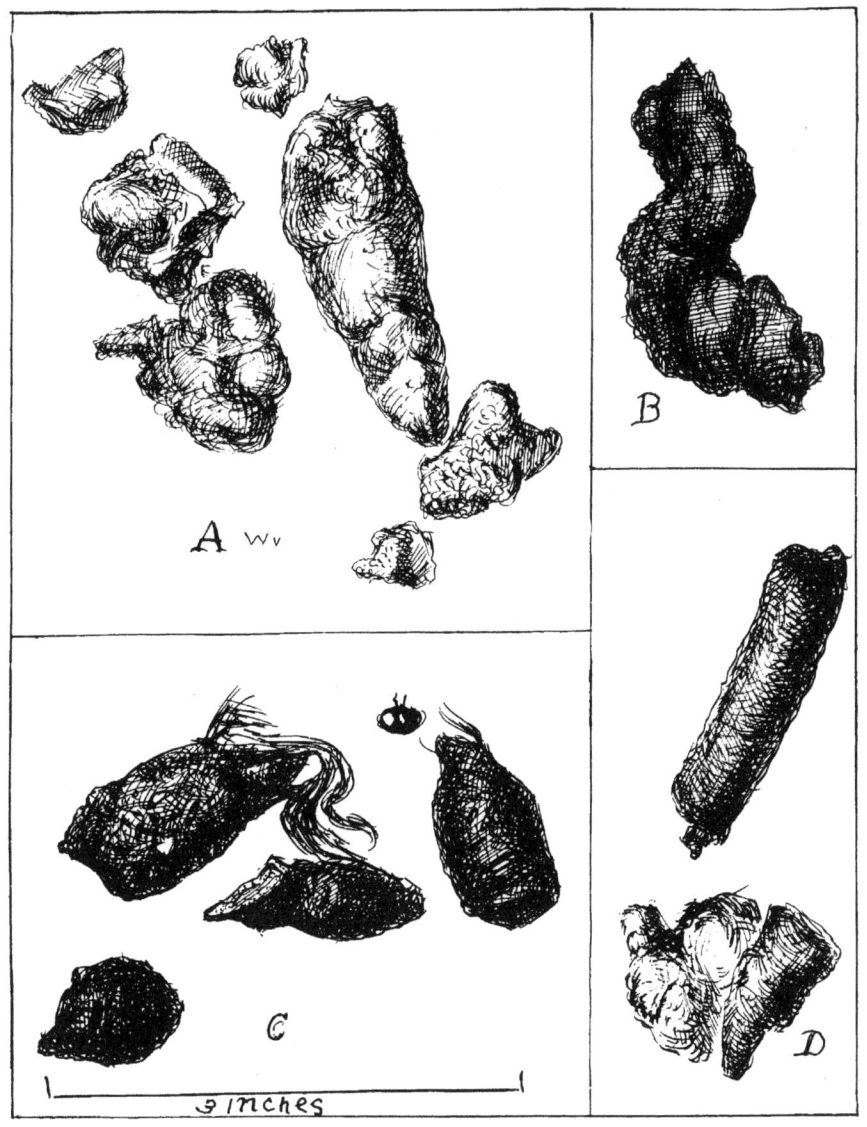

Scatology of certain Mustelidae (all the same scale)
a. Wolverine, Oct. 1908   b. Badger, Oct. 1908
c. Skunk. Chiefly remains of grasshoppers, wasps, but in this case the tail feathers of a small bird also. Cos Cob, Conn., Oct. 10, 1908
d. Fisher, April 28, 1905

animals like the Pocket Gopher and Kangaroo Rat, whose labyrinthine dwellings are equally well equipped with food storerooms and dry-earth sanitation closets.

However, this also is practiced by many Cats—all, I think, whose native surroundings are arid and nearly waterless. When at home, they are accustomed to bury their dung in the sand. In the zoo these are careful at least to deposit it in one corner of the cage, often going through the motions of burying it, though no loose material be available.

In the case of the Cats, we find that they use two, maybe all three, methods. Those species which live in well-watered forests habitually drop their dung in water; and those to whom water is not available, bury it.

Dogs follow the dry plan. They keep their dens clear; and commonly show a disposition to scratch some earth onto their dung deposit. This they do with their hind feet. Likewise, the two or three vigorous scratch marks of the Wolf are often seen near their deposit.

THE PARASITIC SYSTEM

The third plan is, of course, quite unconsciously followed; that is, the fecal output is left exposed to special insect parasites that speedily render it innocuous.

An interesting illustration of this comes to me from Nova Scotia, and refers to the big Wildcat of that Province.

Arthur R. Rice tells me that there is near Digby, Nova Scotia, a long glacial dump. On this are a great many anthills; and on every anthill a Wildcat has left its excretes.

When Metchnikoff, in his *Prolongation of Life*, demonstrated to the world that the lower colon was the breeding place of parasitic flora and fauna, which were probably responsible for man's shortened span of existence, he at least opened a new field of research.

SCATS OR SIGNS

In my *Life Histories*, I demonstrated that no animal can have a home—that is, a prepared, fixed, and permanent refuge from the weather, etc.,—unless it has developed the rudiments of sanitation; which carries with it a *limitation of daily evacuations*. This further implies a great increase in the size and storage capacity of the colon.

To the hunter the "sign" is an important source of information. First, it tells him definitely what species of animal it is that passed this way.

Second, the size of the pellets tells whether it is a large or small specimen of the kind.

Third, if the pellets are all in one pile, it means that the creature was unalarmed, that it had no idea of the hunter's proximity. If they are scattered along a yard or two of trail, it means that the creature was hurrying away.

Fourth, the consistency and temperature of the pellets are all-important. In wintertime, when most still-hunting is done, the expert can, by the condition of the pellets, tell much about the creature's whereabouts. If the pellets are steaming hot, it means that the game is close at hand and well within shot. If the pellets are cold, it means they have been dropped about half an hour before, and the animal may be a mile away. If the pellets are frozen hard, it means that they were dropped over an hour ago, and the quarry is probably a couple of miles away.

THE MUSKRAT POST OFFICE

When a Dog goes up to a lamppost, sniffs it, then leaves his own uric record, it means simply that he is looking up the common register of his people to see if any friend has been this way of late. Then, for the benefit of the next, he puts himself also on record.

Most animals have some such way of communicating with their people.

One of the best-developed and most obvious cases was the Muskrat Post Office that is sketched on page 141, and which I observed on the Ottawa River, forty miles east of Kippewa, Quebec.

I have seen many of these, but this was the most elaborately developed Bureau of Information and Registration that I have observed up to date. Each Muskrat that landed seemed in duty bound to leave his "visiting card" for the benefit of all concerned. The lower right drawing is an enlargement of the group of scats above it on the log; and the lower left represents a similar group observed elsewhere on the Ottawa. All pellets were of a blackish-green color.

Muskrat post office

21 Bear Trees and Other Animal Signs

Every writer who is conversant with Bears in their natural surroundings has much to say about Bear trees. It is well known that all woodland Bears, especially the Black Bear, have certain trees on their range that they use for a number of obscure but very animal purposes.

I have seen a great many of these trees, especially in the Rocky Mountain region. Whenever the Bear, presumably the claimant of this range, comes near a Bear tree, he smells it, much as a Dog does the lamppost; then he attacks it with tooth and claw for a few seconds, and growls savagely as though to warn off all rivals.

The exact purpose of this performance is not definitely settled, but there is no doubt of this: it lets other animals, particularly other Bears, know that this range is already possessed by one of their kind. It says in effect: "If you wish to meet the original settler, hang around; if you don't, you had better clear out!"

The Buck tree figured (page 145) is clearly marked by the

horns of a buck Deer who has recently grown his new set, and is taking advantage of this opportunity to clean off the velvet, and otherwise prepare them for war.

The Porky tree is something I can see any day from the windows of my home in the pinewoods of the Rocky Mountains. The Porcupines, which here abound, are especially fond of the inner bark of a young pine tree. When they climb a tree to make a meal they usually select for comfort a stout, convenient branch on which they sit, while they steady themselves with forepaws, holding onto the main trunk, and easily help themselves to a pound or more of nutritious inner bark.

The drill holes of the sapsucker or yellow-bellied woodpecker are familiar to every farm boy in the East. While it seems most likely that it was a definite desire for sap that caused the woodpecker to drill, there can be no doubt that insects are attracted and trapped by the sweet and ultimately sticky sap; and these are welcomed as a lawful addition to the woodpecker's bill of fare. Orchard trees and quaking asp are the species I have most often seen tapped for this purpose.

Observations seem to prove that the woodpecker taps a whole series of trees; and at mealtime goes around, calling at each and every one of these lunch counters, to feast on the insects captured by the sap, or on the sweet sugary sap itself.

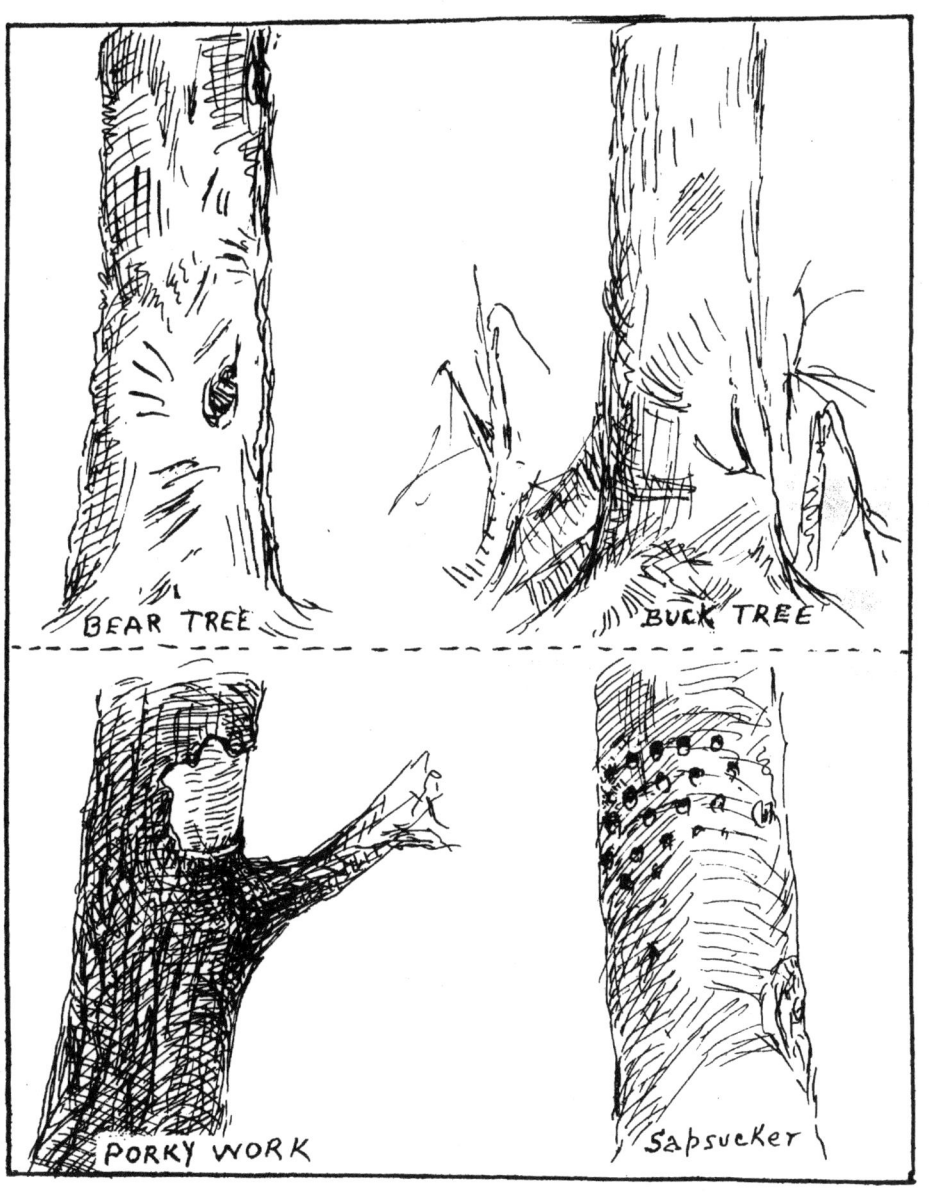

Animal Signs

22 Blazes and Indian Signs

First among the trail signs that are used by Indians and White hunters, and most likely to be of use to the traveler, are ax blazes on tree trunks. Some of these may vary greatly with locality, but there is one that I have found everywhere in use with scarcely any variation. This is the simple white spot meaning HERE IS THE TRAIL (page 149).

The Indian, in making it, may nick off an infinitesimal speck of bark with his knife; the trapper, with his hatchet, may make it as big as a dollar; or the settler, with his heavy ax, may slab off half the tree side. But the sign is the same in principle and in meaning, on trunk, log, or branch, from Atlantic to Pacific, and from the Rio Grande to Hudson Strait. THIS IS YOUR TRAIL, it clearly says in the universal language of the woods.

There are two ways of employing it; one, when it appears on back and front of the trunk, so that the trail can be run both ways; the other, when it appears on but one side of each tree, making a *blind trail*. This can be run one way only, and is often used by trappers and prospectors who do not wish anyone to follow their back track.

But there are treeless countries where the trail must be marked; regions of sagebrush and sand, mountains of rock, stretches of stone, and level wastes of grass or sedge. Here other methods must be employed.

Among stones and rocks, the recognized sign is one stone set on top of another; and in places where there is nothing but grass, the custom is to twist a tussock into a knot.

These signs also are used in the whole country from Maine to California.

In running a trail, one naturally looks straight ahead for the next sign. If the trail turned abruptly without notice, one might easily be set wrong, but custom has provided against this.

The tree blaze for TURN TO THE RIGHT is shown on page 149. The greater length of the turning blaze seems to be due to a desire for emphasis; as the same mark set square on is understood to mean LOOK OUT! THERE IS SOMETHING OF SPECIAL IMPORTANCE HERE.

Combined with a long side chip, it means VERY IMPORTANT; HERE TURN ASIDE. This is often used to mean CAMP IS CLOSE BY; and a third sign that is variously combined, but always with the general meaning of WARNING or SOMETHING OF GREAT IMPORTANCE, is a threefold blaze. The combination would read LOOK OUT NOW FOR SOMETHING OF GREAT IMPORTANCE TO THE LEFT. This is a blaze I have often seen made by trappers to mark the whereabouts of their trap or cache.

Surveyors often use a similar mark, that is three simple spots and a stripe, to mean THERE IS A STAKE CLOSE AT

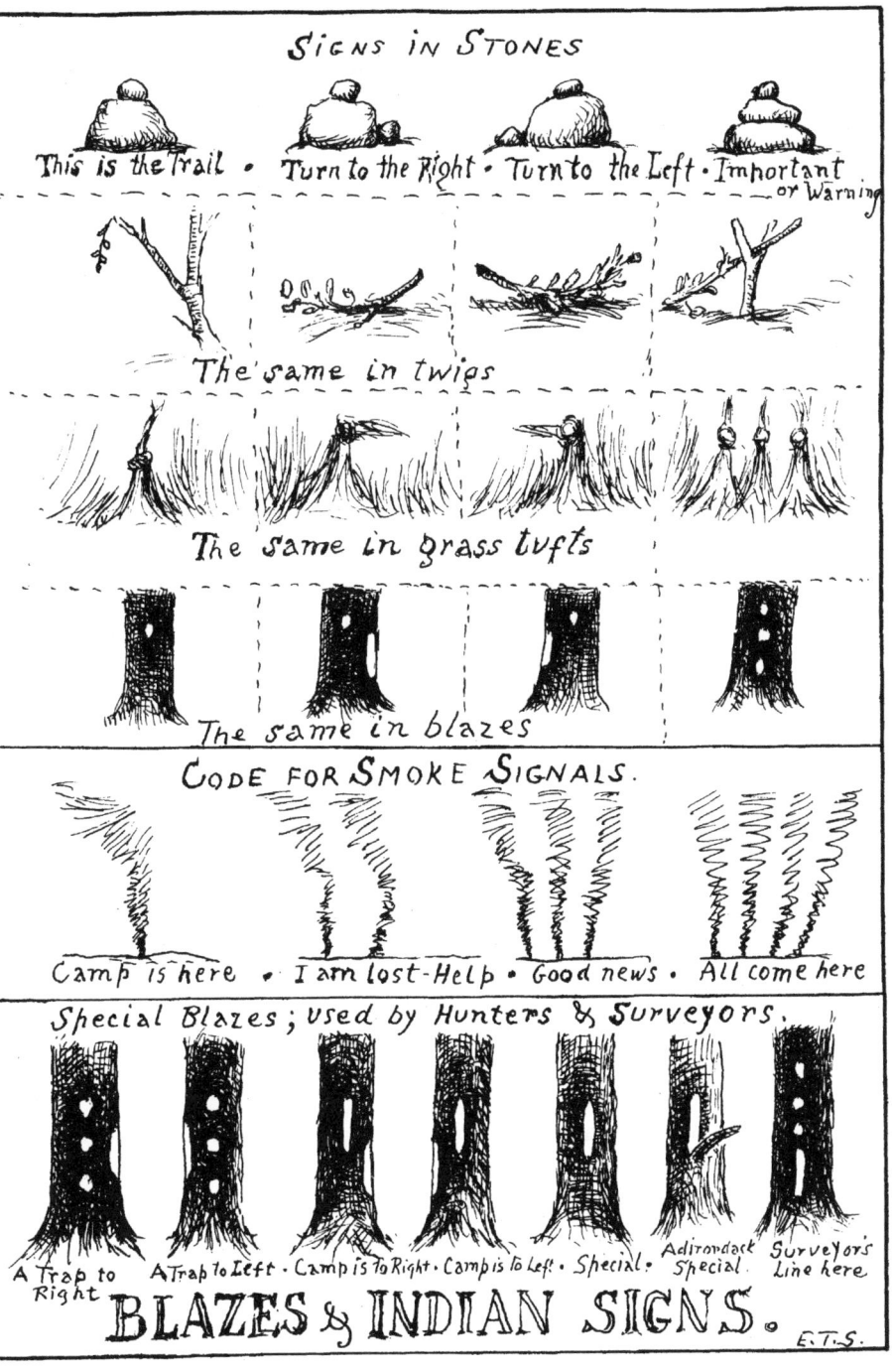

ANIMAL TRACKS AND HUNTER SIGNS

HAND, while a similar blaze on another tree nearby means that the stake is on a line between.

These signs done into stone talk would be as indicated in the drawing.

Of course, the first two are sometimes combined with the last. These are much used in the Rockies where the trail goes over stony places or along stretches of slide-rock. The combination sign is often seen, and would be read: IT IS VERY IMPORTANT TO TURN TO THE LEFT HERE.

Another Indian sign was a little heap of stones to mean, WE CAMPED HERE BECAUSE ONE OF US WAS SICK. This originated in the hot stones used for making steam in the vapor bath that is so much favored by Indian doctors.

In grass or sedge, the top of the tuft is made to show the direction to be followed. If it is a point of great importance, three tufts are tied, their tops straight as in the plate, if the trail goes straight on; otherwise, the tops are turned in the direction toward which the course turns.

THE OJIBWAY TWIG SIGNS

The Ojibways and other Woodland tribes use twigs for a great many of these signs. The hanging broken twig like the simple blaze means THIS IS THE TRAIL. The twig clean broken off and laid on the ground across the line of march means BREAK FROM YOUR STRAIGHT COURSE, AND GO IN THE LINE OF THE BUTT END.

When a special warning is meant, the butt is pointed toward the one following the trail and raised somewhat, in a forked twig. If the butt of the twig were raised and pointing to the left, it would mean: LOOK OUT, CAMP, OR OURSELVES, OR THE ENEMY, OR THE GAME WE HAVE KILLED, IS OUT THAT

WAY. With some, the elevation of the butt is made to show the distance of the object: if low, the object is near; if raised very high, it is a long way off.

These are the principal signs of the trail used by Indians and hunters in most parts of America. These are the standards, the ones that are sure to be seen by the boys who camp in the wilderness.

SMOKE SIGNALS

There is, in addition, a useful kind of sign—the smoke signals. These were used chiefly by the Plains Indians, but the Ojibways also seem to have employed them at times.

A clear, hot fire was made, then covered with green stuff or rotten wood, so that it sent up a solid column of black smoke. By spreading and lifting a blanket over this smudge, the column could be cut up into pieces long or short; and by a preconcerted code, these could be made to convey tidings.

But the simplest of all smoke codes and the one of chief use to the western traveler is this:

One steady smoke: HERE IS CAMP.

Two steady smokes wide apart: I AM LOST: COME AND HELP ME.

I find other smoke signals, namely:

Three smokes in a row: GOOD NEWS

Four smokes in a row: ALL ARE SUMMONED TO COUNCIL.

These latter I find not of general use, nor are they so likely to be of service as the first two given.

GUN LANGUAGE

The old Buffalo hunters had an established signal that is

yet used by the mountain guides. It is as follows:

Two shots in rapid succession, an interval of five seconds by the watch, then one shot means: WHERE ARE YOU?' The answer, given at once, and exactly the same means: HERE I AM: WHAT DO YOU WANT?

The reply to this may be one shot, which means: ALL RIGHT, I ONLY WANTED TO KNOW WHERE YOU WERE. But if the reply repeats the first, it means: I AM IN SERIOUS TROUBLE: COME AS FAST AS YOU CAN.

A rude outline of a man with hat and gun on a tree in the Yellowstone Forest was an Indian's way of warning his friends that the soldiers were coming. And it shows, further, how these signs and blazes may have been the beginning of literature.

HORNS IN THE LIVING TREE

The Indians sometimes marked a spot of unusual importance by sinking the skull of a Deer or a Mountain Sheep deep into a crotch of a living tree, so that the horns hung out on either side. In time, the wood and bark grew over the base of the horns, and a "medicine tree" was created.

Several of these trees have become of historic importance. A notable example was the big Ram Tree that, by common consent, demarked the hunting grounds of the Blackfeet from those of the Nez Percés. It was held by these Indians in religious veneration until some White vandal deliberately destroyed it by way of a practical joke.

It would be easy to record many other Indian signs; for instance, the sign for the first crow of spring, the sign for Buffalo in sight, the sign for a war party coming, the sign

BLAZES AND INDIAN SIGNS

that a certain man wants the arrows that another man owes him, the sign that the owner of the tepee is praying and must not be disturbed.

But these are things that are quickly passing away; even the Indians themselves are forgetting them.

The most important of the signs used by men of the wilderness are herein described. The knowledge of such things appeals to most of our young people; they find pleasure in learning this crudest of writing. And, lest any should condemn it as an idle pleasure, it is well to remember that many a one in the past has owed his life to an inkling of this woodcraft knowledge; and there is no reason to doubt that many a wilderness traveler in the future could find it of equally vital service.

23 Blazes Used in Town

A blaze is a simple mark conveying an idea or information without reference to words or letters. One might suppose that when the White man left his primitive hunter life, and went to live in town, signs and blazes ceased to be of interest or of service to him.

This is far from the fact. Many of the old wilderness blazes did, indeed, drop out of use; but a crop of other codes sprang up under the urge of city traffic, city residence, and city life. In the world of commerce, in the era of the automobile, and of the minute division of real estate, many new ideas had to be blazoned.

It would be possible to show that our printed letters, as well as our numbers, all had their origin in blazes or crude signs invented by primitive man. But that is a far-off subject, and has little relation to the everyday life of the White race today.

The next page illustrates some thirty of the blazes most familiar in our ordinary civilized life.

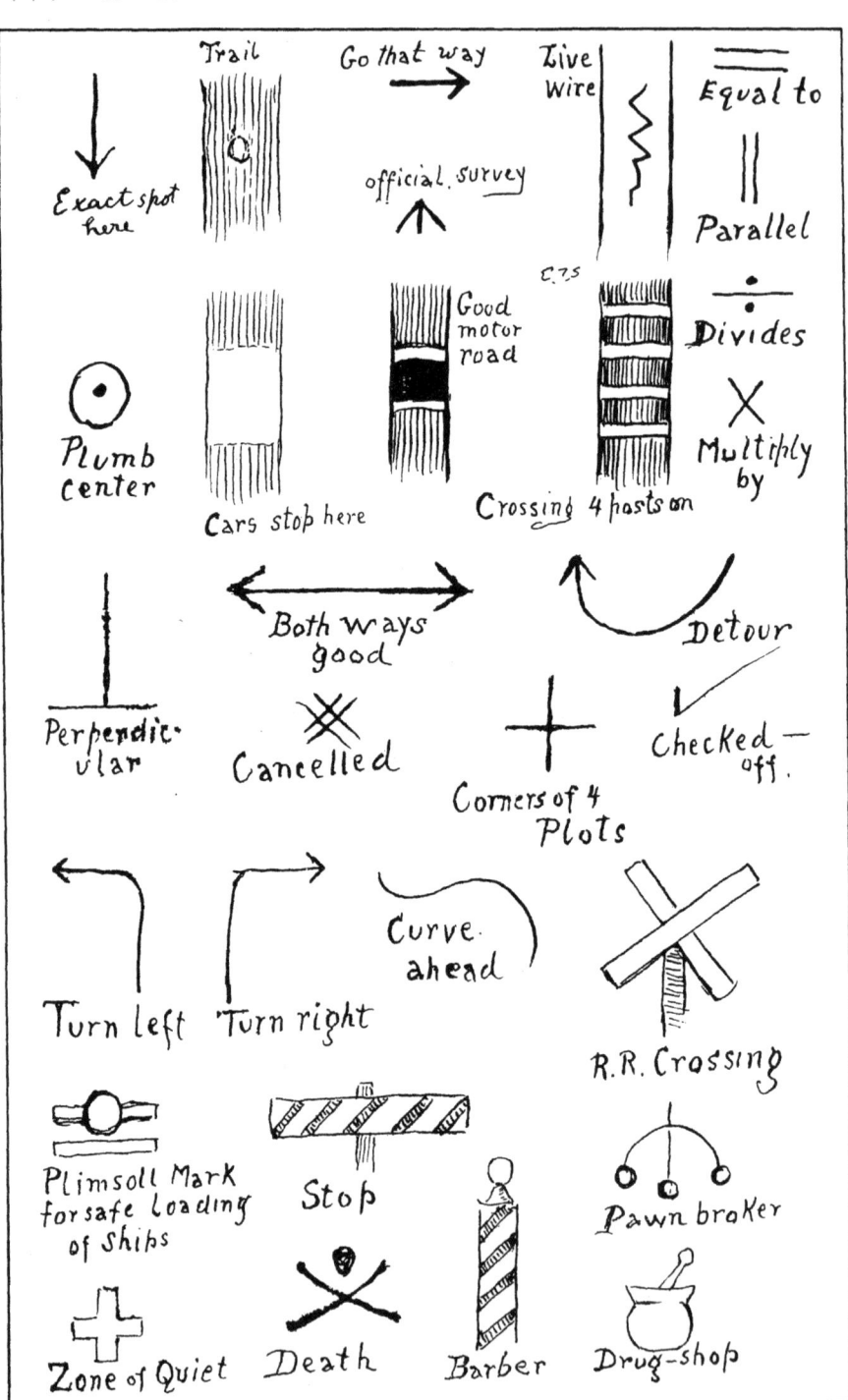

Blazes used in town

A Final Word

For seventy years I have been following the trails of our wild brethren. My notes and sketches are before me now in some fifty fat manuscript Journals, with illustrative drawings that aggregate many thousands. So far as I know, no other naturalist has worked so long or so persistently as I in deciphering and recording the mysteries of the trail.

From these Journals I have drawn the facts and sketches for this small book; and, throughout, I have indeed been embarrassed by the superabundance of the material.

For the benefit of those who wish to follow my method of study in this, the oldest of all writing, I urge that they never lose an opportunity, whether the track be in mud, dust, or snow. Copy it, not from memory, but at the time. And let me again emphasize the idea that sketching is always the handiest method. Be sure to make a series of three or four tracks, with their spacing and alignment—a single track is of much less value. Be sure that it is drawn life-size, or at least to a definite scale which appears on the drawing.

Remember the old adage, "The thing I am seeking is seeking for me"; which, translated, means that if I am devotedly interested in something, that something will come ever more into my life, and afford opportunities that are unknown to those who are blind to such pursuits.

Not only does the trailer become woodwise, but realizes more and more that:

>Wild things write their lives for him
>In endless manuscript.

Index

American Red Fox, 47; black-tracks, 49 (*ill.*); *see also* Red Fox
American Robin, tracks, 114 (*ill.*)
Animals: activity period, 20; northern, 119; sanitation, 136, 138–139
Animal tree signs, 145 (*ill.*)
Antelopes, 116; tracks, 118 (*ill.*)

Barn Yard Chicken tracks, 53 (*ill.*)
Black Bears, 143; tracks, 128 (*ill.*)
Blackfeet, 152; *see also* Indians
Blacktail Jack Rabbits: bedding down 65 (*ill.*); spy-hop, 65 (*ill.*); tracks, 65 (*ill.*)
Black-tracks, 36, 39–40, 42, 44, 47–48, 49 (*ill.*); Microtus, 50 (*ill.*)
Blarina: tracks, 21 (*ill.*); tunnels, 21 (*ill.*)
Blazes, 147–148, 149 (*ill.*), 155, 156 (*ill.*); *see also* Signs
Bobcat Lynx, 107; tracks, 106 (*ill.*)
Brook Turtle tracks, 75 (*ill.*)
Bull Moose tracks, 120 (*ill.*)

Caribou, 132; tracks, 124 (*ill.*)
Cats, 93–94, 138; structure, 54; tracks, 47, 69, 70 (*ill.*), 103, (*ill.*); walking, 54, 56
Cattle, domestic, tracks, 55 (*ill.*)
Coons, 18; tracks, 112 (*ill.*)
Cottontail Rabbits, 59, 60, 102; tracks, 61 (*ill.*), 65 (*ill.*), 76 (*ill.*), 83 (*ill.*); trail, 79 (*ill.*), 85 (*ill.*)
Coyotes, 87, 91, 105; characteristics, 89 (*ill.*); tracks, 53 (*ill.*); 88, 89 (*ill.*); trails, 34

Crow tracks, 29 (*ill.*), 53 (*ill.*)

Deer, 115, 136; tracks, 26, 117 (*ill.*)
Deer Mice, 18; tracks, 21 (*ill.*)
Dogs, 58, 71, 91, 102, 138; tracks, 34, 47, 57 (*ill.*), 70 (*ill.*), 94, 103 (*ill.*); walking, 56
Dry system, 136
Dung pellets, 24, 122 (*ill.*), 133 (*ill.*), 135 (*ill.*), 137 (*ill.*), 141 (*ill.*); *see also* Scats

Elk, bull, tracks, 125 (*ill.*)
English Sparrow tracks, 114 (*ill.*)
European Blackbird tracks, 114 (*ill.*)

Fox, 26, 93–94, 96; brush marks, 71, 94; characteristics, 89 (*ill.*); track cameos, 96; tracks, 5 (*ill.*), 70 (*ill.*), 89 (*ill.*); trails, 70 (*ill.*), 85 (*ill.*), 93–94, 95 (*ill.*); *see also* American Red Fox and Red Fox
Fox Squirrels, 48; black tracks, 50 (*ill.*)

Gray Fox, feet, 35 (*ill.*)
Grizzly tracks, 128 (*ill.*)
Ground-bird tracks, 114 (*ill.*)

Hares, Snowshoe, tracks, 129 (*ill.*); *see also* Rabbits
Hawk tracks, 83 (*ill.*)
Horse tracks, 43 (*ill.*), 45 (*ill.*)
House Rats, 18; tracks, 19 (*ill.*)
Human tracks, 104 (*ill.*)

INDEX

Indians, 17, 18, 51, 52, 147, 151, 152; Blackfeet, 152; Ojibway, 150–151; signs, 149 (*ill.*), 152; Sioux tracks, 103 (*ill.*)

Jack Rabbits, 59–60; tracks, 61 (*ill.*), 67 (*ill.*)

Kit-fox feet, 35 (*ill.*)
Kodiak Brown Bear tracks, 128 (*ill.*)

Least Shrew track, 21 (*ill.*)
Long-tailed Chipmunk tracks, 21 (*ill.*)

Martens' paws, 127 (*ill.*); tracks, 126 (*ill.*)
Meadow-Mouse tracks, 21 (*ill.*)
Microtus, 48; black tracks, 50 (*ill.*)
Mink, 18; tracks, 76 (*ill.*); trail, 79 (*ill.*)
Mole Shrew tracks, 21 (*ill.*)
Moose, 132; tracks, 120 (*ill.*), 121 (*ill.*)
Mountain Lion tracks, 31 (*ill.*)
Mule Deer tracks, 117 (*ill.*)
Mule tracks, 43 (*ill.*)
Muskrats: post office, 139–140, 141 (*ill.*); tracks, 76 (*ill.*), 122 (*ill.*)

Otter tracks, 41 (*ill.*)
Owls, 82, 84; tracks, 83 (*ill.*)

Pig, domestic, tracks, 37 (*ill.*), 38 (*ill.*)
Possums, 18; tracks, 120 (*ill.*)
Prairie Chickens, 97; tracks, 53 (*ill.*)

Rabbits: Cottontail, 59, 60, 102; Jack, 59–60; labels, 60, 63 (*ill.*); *see also* under Name of Animal
Red Fox, feet, 35 (*ill.*); tracks, 47; trail, 34; *see also* American Red Fox and Fox
Red Squirrels, 18; tracks, 19 (*ill.*)

Scatology, 131–132
Scats, 131, 136; *see also* Dung pellets
Sheep, domestic, 116; tracks, 38 (*ill.*)
Shorelark tracks, 114 (*ill.*)
Signals: guns, 151–152; smoke, 151; *see also* Signs
Signs, 131, 139; animal, 145 (*ill.*); twigs, 150–151; *see also* Blazes, Dung pellets and Signals
Sioux Indian tracks, 103 (*ill.*)
Skunks, 18, 105, 107; tracks, 106 (*ill.*), 108 (*ill.*)
Snapping Turtles' tracks, 4 (*ill.*), 75 (*ill.*)
Snowshoe Hare tracks, 129 (*ill.*)
Spooring, 28
Spy-hop, 62, 65 (*ill.*)

Texan Lynx, 47, 71; black-tracks, 49 (*ill.*)
Toad tracks, 29 (*ill.*)
Tracking, ideal time, 24, 26
Track records, 7, 8, 52; black-track printing, 36, 39–44, 47–48; casting in plaster, 34, 36; photographing, 34; sketching, 33–34
Tracks: geographical placement, 30; oldest writing, 17–18, 20, 23; source of information, 24; *see also* under Name of Animal
Trailing, 51–52, 54; animal activities, 32; rules, 28, 30
Trail signs, 147–148

Weasels, 18; tracks, 19 (*ill.*)
Whitetail Deer tracks, 25 (*ill.*), 27 (*ill.*)
Whitetail Jack Rabbit tracks, 65 (*ill.*), 85 (*ill.*)
White Turkey tracks, 21 (*ill.*)
Wolves: characteristics, 89 (*ill.*); tracks, 57 (*ill.*), 58, 88, 89 (*ill.*); trail, 34, 57 (*ill.*)
Wood Buffalo tracks, 123 (*ill.*)
Woodchucks, 18, 19 (*ill.*), 28; tracks, 53 (*ill.*)

Printed by Libri Plureos GmbH in Hamburg, Germany